AF413228

ADVANCE PRAISE

The captivating true story of Rudi's flight from the Nazis and a new life shaped across borders and continents. An evocative, compelling journey of survival against the odds...

   – Dr Helen Fry, historian and author, expert in Second World War British Military Intelligence and Espionage

Rudi Haymann's memoirs are a captivating slice of history. They take the reader on a journey from Berlin to British Palestine, North Africa, Italy, and finally Chile, and paint a vivid image of the places and people Rudi encountered, capturing the readers' imagination and heart, while also allowing them to grin at Rudi's fine sense of humor. The touching letters between Rudi and his family are a special treasure: it's a great luck that they survived the passing of time and the winding paths of life.

   – Sarah Blendin, Stiftung Exilmuseum Berlin

Saying Rudi Haymann's war was unusual would be an understatement. Born in Berlin, he escaped the Nazis, joining the Haganah in Palestine and then the British Army in WWII. Selected to the Intelligence Corps, he initially worked undercover in German POW camps, and then as a frontline Interrogator. His service took him to the front lines in North Africa and Anzio; to Greece with the resistance, and Italy again, capturing high-profile prisoners. Eventually he settled with his family who had escaped to Chile. In 1942 his CO told him he was a "witness to history"; Rudi immediately started a diary which is now this fascinating book of one man's commitment and courage in the fight against Nazism. The Intelligence Corps is extremely proud to count Rudi as a veteran.

– **Colonel (Retd) Nick Fox OBE. Former Deputy Colonel Commandant, Intelligence Corps**

At 27, Rudi Haymann had already lived more lives than most of us will over a whole lifetime. At 102, he recalls those early years. Absolutely gripping, a story of fate, survival, moral choices, and daring across one of the most difficult periods of history. It is the ultimate page-turner and it all actually happened!

– **Josué Tanaka, Visiting Professor in Practice, London School of Economics. Former Managing Director, European Bank for Reconstruction and Development, London**

Rudi, a centenarian, is an extraordinary individual whose personal story has left an indelible mark on my heart. Through Rudi's story, we gain a deeply personal and inspiring perspective on history. His incredible journey serves as a testament to the triumph of the human spirit and the power of resilience.

– **Tamara Donnenfeld. Lifelong Learning Director, Temple Beth Am, Miami**

Rudi Haymann's inspiring life story of resilience takes readers on an extraordinary journey through Europe, Africa, and America, offering a firsthand account of World War II. Through vivid and powerful narration, Haymann skillfully brings the intense emotions and difficult situations he faced, making history meaningful to those who read his testimony.

– Valeria Gómez Meyer. Student at the Freie Universität Berlin. Madricha & Board Member of Hashomer Hatzair Germany

BEYOND BORDERS

ESCAPING THE HOLOCAUST
AND FIGHTING THE NAZIS. 1938 - 1948

RUDI HAYMANN

ISBN 9789493322219 (ebook)

ISBN 9789493322226 (paperback)

ISBN 9789493322233 (hardcover)

Publisher: Amsterdam Publishers, The Netherlands

info@amsterdampublishers.com

Beyond Borders is part of the series Holocaust Survivor Memoirs World War II

CONTENTS

Where do the rivers of memory flow?
Memory, our marvelous gift,
It registers the past and is colored by our present gaze.
Memories of the time I migrated across borders.
A decade of changes, conquests,
sorrows, and wonders.

In memory of my wife Ati and my son Guido.
To my daughters Liora and Dalia,
and my grandchildren Tanya, Gadiel and Dan.

My father, Vati, 1912.

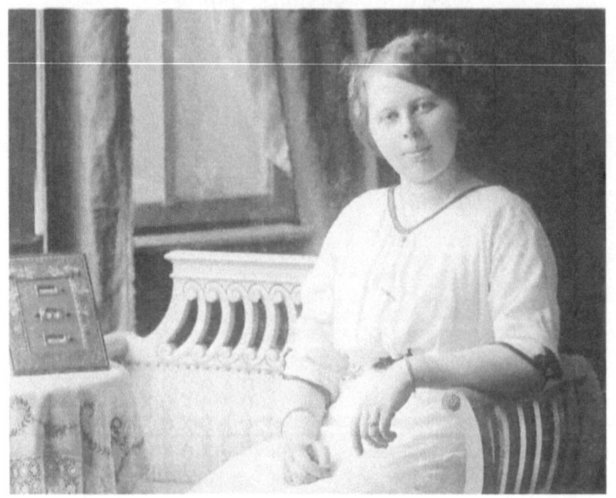

My mother, Mutti, 1912.

THEY ROBBED US OF OUR HOMELAND

BERLIN, GERMANY, 1938

In May 1938 I was summoned to the police station in Berlin and informed that I was "under police surveillance" until I left the country. I was given no explanation. I was stunned. At barely 16 years old, I was being expelled from Germany, the country where I was born, and before me, my parents, and my grandparents. My Jewish family had already suffered intimidations under Nazi rule, but this event greatly alarmed my parents, presaging the terror ahead.

Hitler had ascended to power in Germany in 1933 and had since orchestrated the progressive collapse of Jewish life. His Nazi anti-Jewish policies brought the gradual dispossession of Jewish property, the exclusion of Jews from practicing any profession, the elimination of Jewish rights and even Jewish human dignity. Jewish children were expelled from schools; Jews were prohibited from attending concerts or recreational activities and from using urban public spaces. Jews were forced to wear a yellow star to be easily identified. Life became dangerous and unbearable.

German Jews had fought for Germany in World War I, including my father Ludwig, and his brother Fritz. Ludwig was awarded the Honor Cross in recognition of his service, and Fritz, the Iron Cross. Before them, my grandfather had fought in the

Franco-Prussian war of 1870, contributing to the unification of Germany. Jews had also made notable contributions to the Germany's intellectual, professional, and scientific sectors – Thomas Mann and Heinrich Heine in literature; Schoenberg and Mahler in music; Wittgenstein, Buber, and Bloch in philosophy; Erich Fromm and Fritz Perls in psychology; Max Planck, Max Born, Rudolf Lipschitz, and Albert Einstein in science, Rothschild and Mendelssohn in banking – all of which had forged a strong and proud Jewish-German identity.

In this context, German Jews like my father resisted the idea of abandoning their dear homeland, and held on to the belief that Nazi ideology would soon be overcome.

But by 1938, it only got worse. The circle of Nazi intimidation was closing in on me, on my family, and on all German Jews. Some Jewish families managed to emigrate before total Jewish annihilation. Most did not.

I escaped Germany to British Mandate Palestine in October 1938 and later joined the British Army and fought the Nazis in World War II. My parents and sister managed to escape miraculously to faraway Chile in late 1939 and lived the challenges of refugee life and immigration. Ten years passed before I met my parents again; a decade of changes, sorrows, conquests, and wonders.

This is our story.

BERLIN
GERMANY, 1930–1938

My family lived in Eyke von Repkowplatz, in the Hansa district in Berlin. From our apartment window I could see the crescent shape of the Spree river. My father (Vati) was a chemist-pharmacist and ran the well-known Stein Apotheke in downtown Berlin. My mother (Mutti) came from a Protestant family and had converted to Judaism. I was born in 1921, followed two years later by my sister Hilla. We lived a happy childhood; we went to public schools, played with neighborhood friends, and enjoyed Berlin.

When I turned ten, my father enrolled me at the Oberstädtisches Realgymnasium, a reputed public school in downtown Berlin. We learned science, math, history, geography, and languages: Latin, French, English, and Greek. We had to be men of culture, like our fathers and grandfathers. We learned under strict Prussian discipline; any minor offense was punished. If we yawned without covering our mouth, we had to write "Yawning without covering your mouth is lack of culture" a hundred times. For more serious offenses, we were summoned to the teacher's desk. We had to hold our hands at waist level and the teacher would strike our fingers with a wooden rod. God, it hurt! The fingers swelled and burned for hours. But we knew to raise our left hand imperceptibly higher to receive the blows, saving our right hand to do our homework and avoid another punishment. All this discipline did not diminish our youthful joy and happiness. These were simply the rules of the game.

I have pleasant family memories of those years. The *Herrenzimmer,* our library room, was the coziest space and heart of our home. My father sat in his armchair and read history books and professional magazines, while smoking his pipe. My mother sat at the window, doing needlework. She was warm and loving, and consoled me with sweets when I was punished in school. On weekends my father, my younger sister Hilla, and I went for treks in the beautiful forests and lakes around Berlin. I loved these excursions.

But when I turned eleven in 1933, everything began to change.

Germany had been suffering profoundly from the effects of the Great Depression. The new democracy was weak and incapable of addressing the economic challenges and high unemployment. The people lost faith in the government and political positions became increasingly polarized. In the 1932 elections, none of the political parties was able to form a majority government. In this stalemate, in January 1933, President Hindenburg appointed Adolf Hitler, the leader of the Nazi Party, as the next Chancellor of Germany.

Hitler rapidly transformed the German Republic into a one-party dictatorship. He withdrew from the League of Nations, promoted pan-Germanism, fostered widespread anticapitalism, anticommunism, and antisemitism, and prepared Germany for a new war. His virulent antisemitism was expressed in new laws that isolated, threatened, and impoverished the Jews. The increasing pressures are deeply etched in my memory.

I was 12 when our corner store became a Nazi meeting place. Gangs dressed in their brown uniforms, swastikas, and boots, sang "We will march until it all falls apart; today we own Germany, tomorrow, the whole world." But it terrified me most when they sang "When Jewish blood spurts off our knives, it will be twice as good."

When I turned 13, municipal workers painted one bench in yellow in our park. This bench was, from then on, the only one allowed for us Jews to sit on. The neighborhood children did not want to play with me anymore.

When I turned 14, Jewish professionals were stripped of their degrees. My father, a chemist-pharmacist, was downgraded to sales clerk. My uncle Fritz, an architect, was downgraded to draftsman. Uncle Fridolin, a violinist in the state orchestra, was downgraded to nothing. Our journey to economic deterioration and poverty was ensured.

At 15, I was expelled from my school. Jewish students were no longer allowed to study in public schools. All Jewish teachers were expelled as well, to avoid the "poisoning of the minds of Aryan children." A small Jewish school was organized by our community to care for the expelled students and teachers. I felt better in this school, as I no longer had to endure isolation and insults: "Wretched Jew," "Traitor to the fatherland," "Filthy Jew."

Then the absences began. One day, Daniel did not come to school; he and his family had left Germany. Another day, Hanna did not show up; she returned three days later with sunken eyes. The Gestapo, the Nazi police, had taken her father. Yes, for all of us, when the bell rang at five in the morning, instead of the milkman, it might be the Gestapo in their "Nacht und Nebel" [Night and Fog] operation, arresting Jewish men. Our lives were shrouded in fear.

At that time, I was also searching for my identity. My father's ideals – to be a proud German – made no sense to me. I was a persecuted Jew. I needed my own ideals. I found them in the kibbutz movement, which combined Judaism with the socialist dream and pursued the creation of our own Jewish homeland in Eretz Israel [Land of Israel] through the establishment of collectively owned agricultural communities, called *kibbutzim* (plural). The first kibbutzim had been created in the early 1900s, and the movement was growing, enriched by a vision that integrated a Jewish identity and the ideal of a more egalitarian society. I was inspired by this vision and very tangible model.

When I turned 16, I was summoned by the police. "You are listed as a danger to the security of the country," the sergeant said. "You are now under police surveillance, and must report to us every morning, afternoon, and night, until you leave Germany." I was appalled; I was being expelled from Germany, the country where I was born, and before me, my parents, and my grandparents.

"Get your son out of Germany as soon as possible!" friends urged my father. "Send my schoolboy alone to an unknown destination? Too painful!" he replied. "Better painful than disastrous," insisted my mother. There were intense discussions at home. My father wanted me to complete my school year before leaving. My mother insisted that I leave immediately; no reasoning would override her instincts. "We are Germans! This will eventually pass!" argued my father. It was unbearable for him to consider that Germany, his beloved and proud homeland, for which he had fought in World War I, was no longer a home for his son or for himself. My non-Jewish mother saw beyond my father's unwavering German loyalty and grasped the true Nazi mindset.

What to do? How to get out? Where to? There was an Anglo-American organization that took at-risk children to England. "I do not want to be a refugee child in a charitable institution," I argued. "I will go to Eretz Israel; I will become a pioneer and work on a kibbutz." "That's hard and dangerous," argued my father. "Yes, but it is a dignified life," I said. My father finally accepted. The pressure was mounting; Jewish books were being burned, Jewish men were being imprisoned. I was in great danger.

I prepared for emigration with Aliyat Noar [Youth Immigration], an organization that took German and Austrian children to Eretz Israel, at that time British-ruled Palestine. The process was daunting: obtaining visas and authorizations, procuring a travel permit, an exit passport, payment of large fees, and multiple other requirements from both the German and the British governments. "You will leave by train on the night of October 24," I was informed. "Bring your documents and a backpack you can carry at all times. This will be your only luggage."

Two weeks before my departure, a Gestapo policeman knocked on our door and demanded that I surrender my passport. I knew that if I did, I would never get it back and everything would be lost. I lied: "My passport is in the Italian consulate for my visa." The passport was in my father's desk drawer, but luckily, the man did not start a search. He ordered me to bring the passport within a week, but by then, I had obtained my emigration certificate.

I was lucky, and still safe.

Farewell at Anhalter Bahnhof, Berlin 1938. I am at the center, looking at the camera. Jewish Museum Berlin, Inv.-Nr. FOT 88/500/106/015, funded by DKLB Foundation.

FAREWELL

BERLIN, 1938

You can only swim for new horizons
when you have the courage to lose sight of the shore
William Faulkner, *The Mansion*

On October 24, 1938, I kissed my girlfriend for the last time. I bade farewell to my aunt, my uncle, and my grief-stricken grandmother. She knew this was the last farewell, the very final one.

That night, 150 youngsters aged 15 to 17 and their families gathered at Anhalter Bahnhof, Berlin's train station, for the final parting. I hugged my parents and my sister Hilla for the last time. I was young and did not know how hard it is for a parent to send their son off, not knowing if they will ever see him again.

As the train departed, I looked out the window at my parents' waving hands. Their hands got smaller and smaller, they blurred in a sea of waving hands, and then they merged with the station's lights into a soft glow far out in the distance. The train took a gentle curve and it all disappeared in the dark of the night. I sat in silence, overwhelmed.

But then, someone started singing "Arza Alinu" [To the Land we go] and I joined in. As we traveled, the darkness of my life in Berlin fell behind. I looked forward to our new life, the *Aliyah*, the immigration.

The journey was long and exhausting. We crossed Austria, which had been recently annexed by Hitler. People were smiling and holding large signs welcoming our German train, but their smiles turned sour when they learned that only Jewish children were traveling on this train. The border officials meticulously inspected our minimal luggage, to charge us for smuggling if we carried more than ten German Marks. Our passports would expire in a few minutes; the Nazi government had stripped us of our German citizenship. We carried only temporary passes for the sole purpose of leaving Germany.

We finally crossed into Italy. How different it was! Friendly people received us and took us to a campground in Trieste where we joined other youngsters coming from other German cities. I wrote a card to my parents: "Arrived well in Trieste, Rudi." Only five words to convey that I was well. My parents had seen me depart but had no assurance that I would arrive at my destination.

In Trieste, 400 youngsters boarded the HMHS *Gerusalemme*, headed to Palestine. The nightmare of our life in Berlin was now behind us, and we eagerly looked forward to our unexplored future. I was headed to the hard life of a kibbutz pioneer, a life of challenges and adventures, completely different from my life in Berlin. I was full of illusions and expectations.

For five days we were on the *Gerusalemme*. I was mostly on the upper deck with my *haverim*, my companions, feeling the sea breeze during the day and gazing at the stars at night. On board, we studied Hebrew, Zionism (return to our land), and socialism; we affirmed our convictions; we sang and danced. Out on the horizon, I saw the outlines of Greece and Cyprus, exotic names, but I was focused only on our goal: Eretz Israel and the Aliyah. "You are on your path; you will be a pioneer," were the lyrics of the song we sang on board.

I didn't sleep at all on our last night on board. I stayed up scanning the horizon for the lights of the port of Haifa. Our ship anchored in the bay, and we disembarked on small boats that carried us to shore. How exciting! New sounds, new languages; the buzz, the noise, the colors, the exotic smells, the hot air on my skin! It all ignited my curiosity and my enthusiasm for this adventure.

We completed the immigration formalities and stepped onto the public square. It was buzzing with activity and people of all colors and types: Arabs in *keffiyehs* [turbans] and bloomers; athletic tanned young Jews in shorts; British policemen in formal uniform with an immutable gaze. A cacophony of sounds in Hebrew, Arabic, and English. An exotic mix of aromas. People selling all kinds of products and carrying all kinds of goods in large sacks and bundles. Animals carrying wooden boxes, tools, construction materials, machinery, and produce. Vehicles of all types, crisscrossing the space in all directions in an apparent chaos. Oh, the bustle, the hustle, and the disorder! A scene from *One Thousand and One Nights*! We had arrived.

A voice called us: "Shalom, shalom!" Fifteen rural buses were parked at the square, each manned by a driver and an assistant. We boarded the buses and departed in two caravans: one headed south to the Negev desert, one headed north to the Galilee. I was assigned to the latter. We followed a winding rural road through a rugged and deserted landscape. Every so often, one of the buses left our convoy to take a side road to a kibbutz. We shouted "Shalom, shalom!" until the bus disappeared from our view.

Three hours later, only two vehicles continued the route. On the top of a hill, our driver stopped, and we descended. From the ridgetop we gazed open-mouthed at the steep slope at our feet and the ample valley of the Jordan river, 600 meters below. What an amazing view! The intense green of the valley contrasted sharply with the surrounding dry landscape we had traversed. And down there, embedded in the center of the green valley, was a shining body of water, Lake Kinneret. Three colors had this beautiful lake: green on the west side, reflecting the valley; deep blue in the center, reflecting the sky; and soft sepia on the east, reflecting the desert of the Golan Heights. I could not take my eyes off this wondrous landscape. And someplace within this amazing valley was my kibbutz.

The lake had three names: Lake Tiberias was the Roman name honoring Cesar Tiberius, dating from the time when the Romans established their stronghold in the Land of Judea. Sea of Galilee was the Christian name from the time when Jesus of Nazareth preached here. And long before that, when David was crowned King of Israel in 1,000 B.C., he stood in this same spot where I was now and felt the same fascination: "This lake has the shape of my lute!" he exclaimed. Since then and for 3,000 years, we have called it Lake Kinneret, the Lake of the Lute.

While we enjoyed the view, a truck arrived and parked next to our buses. Six men descended and covered the windows of our buses with metal planks, leaving only two narrow slits on the windshield for the driver to see through. Our driver now sported a pistol, and his assistant a carbine rifle. Two men climbed on top of our buses and barricaded themselves between our luggage. We climbed back on board and were instructed to place our backpacks on the window seats and to sit on the aisle floor. Our little caravan departed, led by the truck with the guards. Security was a constant challenge in the desert. The winding road with its sharp, narrow curves, was a place of frequent ambushes by desert bandits and outlaws.

Halfway down the hillside there was a sign – "Sea Level" – but we continued to descend to the valley floor, 220 meters below sea level. There, we stopped to dismantle the security elements. We had passed the danger zone.

In the valley, there were youngsters like me, working in the fields with their feet in water above their ankles. The valley of Galilee was a huge swamp, and the young pioneers were working to dry it to create land for cultivation. They were "redeeming the land." Despite the intense heat, they wore long pants and sleeves to protect them from the swarms of mosquitoes teeming around them.

This was our new home. A land of contrasts and challenges: a huge dry desert on the highland, and a huge wet swamp in the lowland.

And this challenge was now ours.

Kibbutz pioneers drying the swamps, 1940.

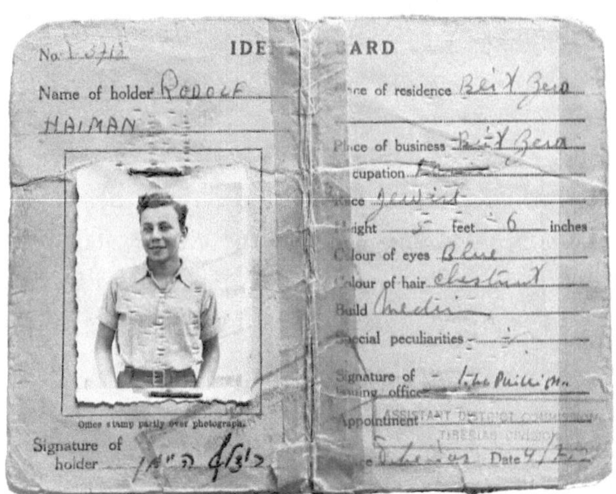

My new Identity Card.

THE KIBBUTZ
BRITISH PALESTINE, 1938

They will plant vineyards and drink their wine;
they will make gardens and eat their fruit.
Amos 9:14

Our kibbutz consisted of seven plain brick houses. One of them was assigned to us newcomers: two bunk beds per room, a table, four chairs, and four lockers for our work clothes. The outer wall of our house was made of reinforced concrete with narrow slits located 12 inches above our beds, to slide our rifles into in case of an attack. We had to be fast and effective: grab the rifle from under the bed, rotate 90 degrees to face the slit, point the rifle through, and be ready to act.

Beyond the houses were our communal buildings: the dining room with its large kitchen, the children's home, a small school building, the infirmary, and the water tank tower with an observation post and two security lights on top. The larger light gyrated at night, scanning the landscape for any suspicious movement. The smaller light was our Morse inter-communicator with other kibbutzim located in the valley. We shared news, data, and calls for help in emergencies. This was our only secure means of communication; we had no phones. The magnet phone was unreliable, as the cables could be easily cut by an attacker.

Farther away were our work areas: the warehouse, the fruit-packing barn, the henhouse, the sheep stables, the dairy, and the cattle barn. Everything was clean and well organized; the dirt roads and pathways were lined with tree saplings which would eventually grow and provide the shade so sorely needed in this harsh climate.

Our kibbutz was surrounded by a barbed-wire fence, a parapet made of sandbags, and trenches. In addition, we built a defense bunker at each of the five corners of our fence. At night, the security lights rotated silently amid the sounds of the gurgling waters of the nearby Jordan river, the howls of the jackals, and the shrieks of the hyenas.

The landscape was beautiful. Our view opened onto the wide valley with its rainbow of greens: the dark green of the swamp and the lighter greens of our fields of oranges, grapefruits, bananas, wheat, and alfalfa. We planted a variety of crops to test product quality and efficacy.

The transformation of this huge swamp into arable land to grow food to feed us and others consumed most of our efforts and energy. How did we dry the swamp? Simple and very laborious. We started on the high end of the valley where the land rose to the hillside; we carved a groove running down; we carved more grooves, a wide network of grooves converging like the veins of a leaf, to a deeper and larger central canal. We worked in the humid heat with handheld hoes, shovels, and picks, digging wider and deeper lines directed down to the bed of the Jordan river. The swamp's water ran through these canals and a beautiful arable earth emerged between the grooves – soft, dark, and rich in nutrients.

For years we worked relentlessly to transform the marshland into a magnificent orchard. The earth was grateful, offering its abundance and fertility after 1850 years of inertia. From the year 135 B.C., when the Romans banned the Jews from their land, countless armies had crossed this land; all wanted to conquer it, but none was willing to work, till, and farm it.

All kibbutz members worked ten hours per day, with three free days per month. In addition, all took turns in security tasks at night in the bunkers or on the observation tower. That was the rhythm of kibbutz life. We, newcomers, had a lighter work schedule for acclimation and learning: six hours of field work, followed by four hours of study each day.

For the first six months, we were assigned to work rotations, to train us and to assess our strengths and likings. The physical work in the fields was exhausting and overwhelming. We had been raised in a cold climate and an urban lifestyle, and we were now suddenly thrown into the heat and the humidity of the swamp, into tight communal living and crushing physical labor. We were absolutely not trained for this. The work chapped the skin of my hands which erupted in blisters and sores; my muscles hurt; my white skin burned. The climate was implacable, with temperatures of over 48 Celsius (118 Fahrenheit), and no air conditioning, of course. Water dripped down my face and my body as I worked, and I could not tell if it was my sweat or my tears of pain. But we all developed and adjusted. Our muscles got stronger, our hands formed callouses, our minds learned, and we all found our paths.

In his first letter to me, my father had written: *"Merke dir Rudi, die Arbeit ist die heiligste Pflicht des Menschen."* [Remember Rudi, work is man's most sacred duty]. Other German parents had conveyed similar concepts to their migrating sons and daughters, reflecting the German values and culture. But our kibbutz mentor said, "Work is self-realization; through our work we affirm our life mission daily." These were not empty words, they reflected the essence and reality of kibbutz life, which our elder *haverim*, our companions, practiced day to day. I was impacted and awed by these amazing people. Their values, their ethics, and their daily example motivated me then, and have guided me throughout my entire life. They are a leitmotif in my life even today, in my very old age.

I had left Germany full of hope for a new life as a farmer. After six months on the kibbutz, I realized I did not enjoy agriculture, and preferred working with animals in the dairy farm. I decided to specialize in dairy and learn its techniques: feeding, milking, insemination, milk production, and grazing methods.

Every afternoon, after field work, we studied. Our studies focused on four topics: Judaism, socialism, agronomy, and self-defense. The first two topics, Judaism and socialism, formed the ideological foundation of our life on the kibbutz. By deepening our understanding of these two sources, we renewed the energy that moved us and we built the mental strength needed to sustain us in such harsh life conditions.

Our Judaism studies focused on the reinterpretation of the Tanach, the Jewish Bible, from a modern perspective and through the lens of social values. We were clear in our minds and hearts that we had to build productive socialism; we had to farm the land, increase production, and expand science, technology, and our own entrepreneurship. We had to create wealth, knowledge, and resources because virtuous socialism should distribute new wealth created. Socialism that does not create new resources and wealth distributes only poverty, has no future, and was not what we were working for.

The third topic we studied intensely was agronomy. Physical effort alone would not create wealth and wellbeing for all. We had to apply technique and technology based on science and experience; we had to innovate constantly. We experimented, we tested crops, and tracked performance statistics to improve the quality and quantity of our production.

The fourth topic we studied was self-defense, a critical skill which was essential to survival in those days. Armed with rifles, we became experts in the "five seconds" technique. First second: throw yourself onto the ground on your left side, using your arm to soften the blow; with your right arm, grab the gun belt and pull it down your shoulder. Next second: roll over on the ground and place your rifle in position. Third second: load the bullet, aim, and place your finger on the trigger. Fourth second: assess your position: Are you uphill or downhill from the attacker? Is the sun in front or behind? Fifth second: check in with your companions: Who will contain the attackers? Who will call for help?

I had a hard time staying awake during our afternoon lessons. Every part of me ached; the tough physical labor consumed all my energies, and my body begged to rest. But we tried our best. We wanted to be like the elder members of our kibbutz and live a meaningful life, transforming an ideal into action.

We had so many expectations and we faced so many challenges! Life on the kibbutz was inspiring but significantly harder than I ever imagined, not only because of the exhausting physical effort and the climate, but also because of the health threats hidden in the swamp: typhus, malaria, and pappataci fever. Contracting these diseases was inevitable; what was most important was to get a rest period between each, to regain the strength to ride the next one. Our companion Selma contracted typhus and soon after, malaria; her weakened body could not resist the double bout and she died at barely 16 years of age.

We also had to handle the challenges of communal life. We lived in an extremely tight physical space – four energetic youngsters per room – in a very regimented lifestyle that lacked ample vital space for each one to fully develop our diverse personalities. This caused some conflicts and triggered deep questioning. After a year on the kibbutz, it became clear how each one of us valued kibbutz life differently. For some, this was the meaningful life they wanted to live, and they fully immersed themselves in the community. Others realized that this lifestyle was not for them, not because of the physical labor, but because they felt their individuality inhibited by the need to conform to the collective.

Myself, I was ambivalent. I wanted to live this experience for some more time to allow my feelings to fully develop. I found it challenging to adjust to the intense collective life, which forced me to contain personal interests in favor of the group. Collective life permeated everything. Even the clothes we wore were shared; they were washed weekly in the communal laundry and redistributed for use. Being a romantic, I felt challenged by the contempt for romanticism in our relations with our female companions, which was part of the "revolutionary mindset" that pursued total equality in gender relations.

Our food was also very different from what we were used to. On the kibbutz we had a light snack at dawn and then ate our main meal – a huge breakfast – at mid-morning, after working in the fields for many hours. Borsht, olives, eggplant, cucumbers, peppers, onions, smoked and pickled fish, eggs, cheese, and strained yogurt were the basis of our kibbutz diet: very healthy, but I missed some of my German food. Familiar food is comfort for the soul.

Life on the kibbutz was not only work and study; it was also very rich intellectually. We all contributed to our community with our own talents or passions. Some formed a choir, others a literary circle, and some worked on the kibbutz's financial planning or in politics. We could join any group based on our personal interests, or could propose any new initiatives – practical or ideological –to the General Assembly on Saturday afternoons.

Sometimes, the kibbutz elders identified a member's particular talent or skill. It was thus that I was invited to join our Security Committee, and received intense training in security and defense by the Haganah, the Jewish self-defense organization that existed during the British Mandate in Palestine.

LETTERS FROM BERLIN

1938-1939

Letters that tell only half-truths also tell half-lies.

On the day of my arrival to the kibbutz, I received the first letter from my father:

> *In the same train in which you leave us, dear son, travels this letter. The last greeting from your old homeland, the first greeting in the new land. Your youth closes today, my son. From now on you will take your future in your own hands. How I would like to be at your side to watch you grow and improve yourself! Whatever life begets us, I promise that I will fight with all my strength to reunite our family again. We are, and will be, father and son. I will deeply miss your conversations. But now, we must walk the arduous path of the Jews... You are our only son, and our future rests on you: keep your integrity. Send us your news. Any news will fill our hearts, a signal from you. Take care of yourself, my son. I love you more than I can express. Your Vati.*

I kept this letter among my personal treasures, but I chose not to re-read it for several years. My father's words overwhelmed me. I did not want him to watch over me, not even with his best intentions. I was 17 and wanted to do it all by myself, to be responsible, and to explore life on my own. *"Our future rests on you."* Heavy words were these; I wanted nothing to hinder the spreading of my wings.

We gathered every night in our kibbutz's communal dining room, around the only radio we had. We heard terrible news. On November 9, 1938, a wave of violent anti-Jewish riots was orchestrated throughout Germany and Austria. In 24 hours of terror, Nazi hordes torched Jewish synagogues, plundered and smashed the windows of Jewish businesses, razed Jewish cemeteries, and abused, assaulted, and imprisoned Jewish men, taking them from their homes. It was called *Kristallnacht* or "Night of Broken Glass," alluding to the shards of broken glass that littered the streets the next day. The terror also shattered Jewish existence in Germany, erasing any remaining hopes that Nazi xenophobia would recede. Kristallnacht made it very clear to all Jews that Nazi policy towards them would entail not only economic and juridical persecution but also naked violence. "The Jew will not survive in Germany," said Heinrich Himmler, leader of the Nazi SS.

What had happened to my own family on that terrible night? My parents had promised to write to me regularly, but I received no news from them. After a long delay, a letter from my mother finally arrived, but it had no words from my father.

Rudi, do not worry about your father not writing to you today; he is very busy.

Why did my father not write to me as usual? What was my mother hiding from me? I anguished and fretted.

Years later, I learned that my father was on his night shift at the pharmacy that night and was alerted on time not to return home. Fearful, he circulated throughout Berlin all day long, avoiding the places where he might be identified. Mrs. Glaser, a neighbor, called my mother in sorrow to let her know that her husband had been taken by the Nazi police. She then offered her home for my father to hide, assuming the police would not return there. Three days later, when the situation calmed down, my father returned home. Mr. Glaser never did.

Not only was my father saved that night; I was saved as well. Had I not left Germany, I would surely have been taken by the Nazis. I was already under police surveillance before leaving, I was already on a list. What good instinct my mother had in insisting that I leave Germany immediately! My non-Jewish mother saw beyond my father's unwavering German loyalty and grasped the true Nazi mindset.

Only after that terrible night did my father accept that there was no return to the Germany that he was so proud of. Only then did he start to actively search for a way to leave the country. He agreed to sign up my sister Hilla to Aliyat Noar, the youth Aliyah organisation. This was illegal and very dangerous, but it was the only option to get her out.

On the kibbutz, we continued to wait anxiously for news. Letters with terrible news arrived, and other letters failed to arrive. We examined each envelope, each stamp, with piercing eyes, trying to guess its content before opening it. The letters reflected the growing anguish of those still trapped in Germany and described their desperate efforts to get a visa, to find asylum somewhere, anywhere. Few countries were open to receive desperate Jews, stripped of all their assets.

Life became an agony for Jews in Germany, marked by social isolation, constant intimidation, loss of jobs, financial hardship, and anguish. The letters conveyed this, but not through direct words. They told half-truths and half-lies, hidden behind words carefully chosen under a double censorship: the Nazi censorship obscuring the true facts, and my parents' self-censorship, as they tried not to increase the worries of their faraway son. But the news filtered through anyway. My distress increased, and my inability to help from afar enraged me to no end.

My dear son: Your letter from Brindisi arrived. Our hearts beat faster with your news. These have been sad and difficult days for us. But I do not want to complain; I clench my teeth and keep going. Hopefully, it is easier for you; a new country and new emotions may help you forget sour memories and help you create a new vision for your future.

Dear son: Unfortunately, I have no contacts who may help us, and I cannot demonstrate that I have 1,000 pounds abroad to obtain an immigration permit to British Palestine. There are no visas available to anywhere in the world.

Dear son: We have been instructed to leave our apartment; they don't want Jews in our building anymore. We must move, we have no choice. We found a smaller apartment, which we do not like, but we must adjust. We had to give away most of our furniture, the armoires, and the piano. There are fewer and fewer Jewish people around us. The Solomons and Gottheimers have left; the Kantarowitzs are about to depart. Farewells have become our devastating destiny.

Dear son: Uncle Fritz and your Oma moved yesterday; Uncle Fritz is no longer allowed to live in his home. We sat Oma on a chair and two strong men carried her down the stairs. Imagine how scared she was!

Dear son: I am not working as a chemist anymore. I am learning upholstering now. Hans is becoming a carpenter, and Lutz, a locksmith. I must be able to work and make money, to reunite the family in the future.

The Nazis prohibited Jews from working in the civil service, exercising their professions, or owning any enterprise. My Uncle Fritz, an architect for Berlin's Central Bank, lived in a building for bank employees that he had designed. The Nazis rescinded his professional title and his right to housing. My father's chemist title was rescinded as well. Seeking to survive, Jewish professionals turned to manual trades, as described by my father.

Every Jew was forced to carry a *Kennkarte*, an identification card with a large red "J" on the front for "Jude" [Jew]. To add humiliation, personal identities were annulled by forcing each man to be named "Israel" and each woman "Sarah" in their documents.

My non-Jewish mother was summoned repeatedly by Nazi officials, who pressed her to divorce my father. However, she was firm in her commitment to her family and never hesitated to follow the uncertain path of the Jews. In the most difficult moments, she held her moral strength, in stark contrast to her physical fragility.

After much anxiety, nine months later, I received an exciting letter:

Dearest son: Incredible news! All has happened quite unexpectedly. I had written countless letters to many consulates trying to obtain a visa to any country, but never received a positive response. I applied to the "Comite de Socorros de Chile," but the application was not acknowledged. I wrote again in Spanish with the help of a translator. Their response: "No applications accepted until July." I also tried Bolivia and Shanghai. I talked to my friend Dossmar, who promised to include us in their application lists. And then, last week, I received a letter advising that a visa to Chile had been authorized for Mutti, Hilla, and myself. What a miracle! This is all thanks to Dossmar. You can't even imagine our happiness and our gratitude! We have visas, finally!

My parents had managed to obtain a visa! It did not matter where to; what mattered was that they had an opportunity to save their lives. I knew little about Chile, a faraway country on the Pacific Ocean, but I blessed it for taking in my little family. Horrible news from Germany continued to pour in, but it was more bearable for me, as I knew my parents had a chance to get out.

But many hurdles had yet to be overcome. Obtaining a visa was only the first step. Now my parents had to get a passport. "You want a passport, Jew?" asked the Nazi bureaucrat. "Did you pay the *Judenabgabe*, the special tax imposed on Jews for sacking the German nation for decades? You want to leave Germany? You must also pay the *Reichsfluchtsteuer*, the exit tax imposed on those leaving Germany. Expensive? Sell your home, your heirlooms, your Sabbath candelabra too." A home was dismantled, a life uprooted, and a few possessions packed in the two suitcases allowed per person.

They also had to procure a space on a ship to South America, a most challenging task. Thousands were anxiously seeking to leave Europe after Kristallnacht – to South Africa, Kenya, Shanghai, Mexico, wherever possible. All destinations were accessible only by ship, and spaces were scarce, extremely costly, and traded on the black market with bribes.

Dear son: I sold our family properties in Ratibor. I was forced to sell them for a ridiculous price to a buyer forced on us by the Nazi government. My father's, mine, and my brother's lifetime work is gone with this sale. For 60 years our family owned these two houses, and they were to be yours one day. Your Oma was devastated. Everybody is touched, but we have no choice. With the funds, I will pay taxes, buy passports and travel tickets, and pay the Committee for Jewish Emigration in Paris. We also must pay the 1,800 Mark Judenabgabe, the tax the Nazis imposed on us Jews.

But once we are settled in Chile, I will call you, beloved son, to my side. I read in your letters that you worry greatly about us. The good news of our visas to Chile may bring you some comfort. I want to take my brother Fritz with us but have been unable to obtain a Visa for him and your Oma. A thousand kisses from your Vati.

My sister Hilla wrote:

Nothing can fail now! We can finally leave Germany. I am sure we will find some work over there. Rudi, a travel permit arrived for me too, and I had to decide whether to go with our parents to Chile or go with the Youth Aliyah to join you in Palestine. I do want to join you with all my heart, but I don't have the courage to leave our parents on their own... So, with a torn heart, I decided to go with them. You can't even imagine how much I struggled over this! I did not share my conflicting emotions with our parents. Going with them, I will be able to help them in that new place.

And then, everything changed completely.
Hitler's troops invaded Poland on September 1, 1939, and Great

Britain and France promptly declared war in response. World War II began. All German frontiers and ports closed; no ships were allowed to leave from German ports. What would happen to my family now? My anguish turned into terror. "Nothing can fail now," Hilla had written. Everything could fail; all had failed.

The letters now featured two censor seals: one German, one British, two nations at war. The news went from bad to worse. The German Army advanced across Europe. What did this mean for my family and for all the Jews still trapped in Nazi Germany? The next letters tersely expressed their fear and desperation:

Dear son: From now on we will only write you open postcards to minimize censor control. All emigration plans are now on hold. We do not know if or when we can leave. Only heaven can help us now... Your Vati

On December 8, 1939, I received a letter postmarked in Italy. I anxiously ripped it open. My parents had left Germany!

My dearest son: We are in Genoa, about to board a ship to South America. We are finally on our way to Chile. Life in Berlin had become extremely hard and dangerous for us... We are economically and emotionally completely devastated. A new life commences now for us. What it will bring, and how we will fare, we do not know. Your letters will now take longer to reach us, Rudi, but now I can hope that I will see you again sometime in the future. Love, from your Vati

Hilla wrote:

Dearest Rudi: We have finally made it! We are about to board the Augustus. Envision our emotion and our excitement. I will celebrate my birthday on a ship! I am immensely grateful to have left Germany; it is extremely dangerous for Jews there now... We were under unimaginable tension. We did not know if, when, or how we would be able to leave. Our emotional strain was intensified because we could not talk about this with anybody; all arrangements had to be carried out in utmost

Germany was already at war and its borders were closed. How did my parents manage to leave? Britain and France had declared war on Germany immediately, but Italy delayed its own declaration, and its frontier remained still open for two months. My parents crossed the border during that short window of opportunity, and boarded one of the last three ships that left Italy for America.

On December 2, 1939, my family boarded the *Augustus* as third-class passengers to their destination, Chile.

DREAMS AND IDEALS
BRITISH PALESTINE, 1939–1941

If I am not for myself, who will be for me?
And if I am only for myself, who am I?
And if not now, when?
Hillel, Pirke Avot 1:14

Hard work, scarcity, and isolation marked our kibbutz life, but this did not diminish our hunger for culture. An old truck with a mobile cinema came to the kibbutz twice a year. We all sat on the lawn in front of our dining hall to enjoy the movies on the roll-out screen. Oftentimes, the Hebrew subtitles did not correspond to the action on the screen, or the film would tear and had to be interrupted to be repaired; but we did not mind: we loved our movies anyway.

A year later we built an open-air amphitheater at a nearby kibbutz, where we enjoyed performances by the Habimah Theater and other groups from Tel Aviv that toured the valley. But we wanted more; raised in a European intellectual environment, we hungered for culture, and we formed our own music and literature groups with talented people from the valley.

But our most frequent source of entertainment was debate. We debated constantly, not because of entrenched disagreements but as an endless, low-cost intellectual activity. Everything was open for discussion: the everyday, the ideological, or the divine. I was young, and my Hebrew was not yet advanced enough to fully participate in the discussions on Judaism, literature, Tanach, or political thought, but I loved to listen and learn. Everything was discussed, except three topics: the weather (hellish), physical work (exhausting), and security (for experts only).

Through these debates, I realized that those of us coming from Germany were quite secular Jews compared with our companions from Eastern Europe, Lithuania, or Russia. We now had to rediscover and reinterpret our Judaism. Our parents' and grandparents' century-long and deep assimilation into German culture had not sufficed; the Nazis had expelled us anyway. Integration is a two-way road: it requires integration from one side, and receptivity from the other.

We discussed what kind of Judaism to cultivate. We were not interested in a religious focus; instead, we chose to reinterpret the Tanach, the Jewish Bible, from the perspective of its historical foundation and its social messages. We also incorporated an agricultural meaning into our Jewish religious festivities to link them to our new rural reality. We wrote our own Passover *Haggadah* celebrating the liberation from servitude in Egypt by linking it to our own escape from Nazism..

We also changed our German names to Hebrew names. Some adopted their given Hebrew middle name. Others chose a completely new name; that's what I did. My parents had given me the middle name Shlomo in memory of my grandfather, but I had never met him and did not feel a real bond with that name. I decided to call myself Gad, the name of the Israelite tribe that had lived centuries ago in this same Jordan Valley where I was living in now. Gad became my new name then, and it is the name my grandson carries today.

For us, socialism was a real way of life rather than an intellectual socioeconomic position. We were not rebelling or building barricades; rather, we chose to be active workers on the kibbutz or in cities. We walked our talk. We had ventured into this land to create life and prosperity out of nothing; we came to till the land with our own hands, to dry the swamps, to green the desert, to create industries, to create schools, to create music and art.

What drove us to work so hard, fight malaria and bandits, drain swamps, and plant trees? A determination to create our own nation, to create the opportunities for self-determination that other people took for granted. We would be not passive observers but active creators of our own history.

The kibbutz was a direct and personal implementation of the ideal of community life: "Everyone contributes according to their potential and receives according to their need." That was our belief, and we practiced it day by day. Our companions Sam and Georg, one small and weak, the other broad-shouldered and strong, worked every day plowing the fields. Georg advanced more than Sam, but their will and effort were the same. Both had the same right to food, shelter, and culture. This was social justice, lived and realized. We wanted to create a better world. We trusted we could do it based on our two guiding principles: social justice and Zionism. We felt that our socialist dream was on the threshold of realization; we were a real and effective example of it. Our dream for a Jewish homeland seemed far more challenging to us. We could not foresee at that time that this dream would become a reality ten years later, and that the socialist ideal would gradually fade away.

Such are the twists and turns of life and of history.

The prophet

My friend Sigi and I worked as cowherds. I loved Sigi; he was 11 years older than I and had a degree in history. He set himself to mentor me to complete my unfinished high school education. Every day at sunrise, we grabbed our guns, opened the cattle corral gate, and guided our herd of 120 cows down the hillside to the river. We crossed the river at a narrow bend, and then climbed up the gentle slope on the other side and let the cattle graze. From this higher point we had a wonderful view over the whole valley and a good tactical defense position in case of an attack by bandits.

That risk was ever-present, but we enjoyed many quiet, beautiful days. At midday, when the sun was at its zenith and the temperature rose above 40 degrees, the herd lay down to sleep and Sigi and I stayed awake with fascinating conversations and Sigi's stories from the Tanach:

> In biblical times this beautiful and fertile valley was called Gush Hallab, the milk-valley. But the valley's inhabitants were very poor. Why? Because wealth was concentrated in the hands of a few landholders. Prophet Amos, a cowherd like us, traveled across the valley preaching for social justice, using a metaphorical language for his peasant audience. He talked about the "fat cows of Beit Sham," meaning not the animals but the plump wives of the rulers. He advised about the wrath of God and the risk to the nation from neighboring enemies. The people of Israel did not have an army at the time and relied on troops of volunteer peasants. But would the peasants close ranks behind their leaders, if the leaders were exploiting them? In prophet Amos' words, God represented social justice. When prophet Amos crossed this valley denouncing injustice, he may have sat on this same rock we are sitting on today.

I was fascinated by the parallel that Sigi was describing. He was teaching me a message of continuity and renewal, of return to our Jewish cultural and national independence. We were now recreating our national identity under a new social structure, after 1,850 years of life in diaspora. The Tanach is the story of our heritage, and we took it as our responsibility to reinterpret it appropriately for our times and our circumstances.

To project ourselves into the future with a vision, we must have a clear understanding of our history; both, vision and history, then become a framework within which to act in our present.

The "Song of Songs"

One day at high noon, when the sun was burning hot and my cattle had lain down to rest, I decided to visit some friends in a neighboring kibbutz. And there, I saw Lotti. Dark hair, a shy smile, and the bluest eyes, shining bright when she glanced up. I was captivated. From that day on, I visited her every Saturday at noon to talk and get to know each other. I departed from my kibbutz freshly showered, hair combed, wearing the only clothes I had: my khaki pants and a blue shirt with a white string instead of buttons, as it was then styled. Lotti's kibbutz was just a 20-minute walk away across the fields, but the midday heat spoiled my careful preparations. Sweat ran down my forehead and my neck, and my shirt got wet and stuck to my body. I wasn't Lotti's only suitor, and the others didn't like my intrusion. As I walked between the kibbutz tents to Lotti's tent, the other youngsters greeted me, mockingly chanting the "Song of Songs," King Solomon's classic and beautiful love poem:

> The voice of my beloved! Behold he comes, leaping over the mountains, jumping over the hills. My beloved is like a deer; looks like a fawn.

Yes, I conquered Lotti. We became good friends for three years. But then, Rommel and his Afrika Korps arrived in Africa, and I left the kibbutz to fight in the war. Four years later, when I returned, Lotti was married to another man.

But the wonderfully gracious words of the "Song of Songs" are with me to this day.

WORLDS APART

BRITISH PALESTINE, 1939–1941

Behold, days are coming
when the plowman shall overtake the reaper,
and the treader of grapes him who sows seed.
Amos 9:13

And then, disaster descended on our kibbutz like a storm in the desert: disease.

The highly infectious foot-and-mouth disease had already infested and killed the cattle in Syria and Transjordan, only four kilometers from our fields. We knew it would reach us, and we prepared for its onslaught by scrupulously disinfecting our animals, establishing quarantines, and keeping our herds away from the open fields. But the disease crossed all physical and political boundaries and stormed into our small community like a furious hurricane. In less than two weeks we lost half of our cattle. This was a terrible blow to our hard work, our sacrifices during all these years, and our scrupulous precautions.

Yes, it was a disaster for us, but it was even worse for our Arab neighbors in the village of Abadiyah. The village *fellahin* [peasants] already suffered poverty before the disease, but there is always another step in the descent to hell.

I observed that the customs and regulations of biblical times described in the Tanach perfectly fit the landscape, the climate, and our experiences in this land. The more I learned from the Tanach, the more I appreciated the wisdom of the ancient texts. In the Third Book of Moses the leaders prepare their people for a life as farmers. They establish practical rules concerning the distribution of land and the rights and obligations for a harmonious communal life. One of these rules is the well-known precept of *Kashrut*: "You shall not boil a goat in its mother's milk" (Exodus 23:19). This rule was essential to protect the lifecycle of domestic animals and prevent their extermination, leaving a family to hunger. Another rule prevents the overexploitation of animals: "You shall not plow mixing an ox and a mule" (Deuteronomy 22:10), because in using animals of unequal strength, you overwork both: the mule will be exhausted trying to match the ox's strength, and the ox will work double to cover for the mule.

Yes, plowing with uneven animals was unwise. But to our horror, we saw that Abadiyah's *fellahin*, who had lost their oxen to the disease, now paired their mules with their wives to pull the plow, directing them with their whips and shouting "*Yallah!*" [Hurry up!]. The poor *fellahin* had no other recourse, as they were forced to produce the crop they owed to their *effendi*, the Arab patron of the land they lived on and to whom they were indentured. Our blood ran cold in the face of a social structure of prebiblical customs.

These situations triggered many discussions on our kibbutz. We examined our conscience and decided we had to act beyond our own community.

At the far end of the Jordan Valley there were new orange plantations on land owned by English and Americans who lived abroad. The plantations were managed by local administrators who contracted Arab foremen, who in turn employed Arab crews and directed them through shouts, insults, kicks, and whips. We decided to show these exploited men that they could demand human decency. We offered ourselves as laborers at the plantation, forming a 12-member crew without a foreman. Each of us was given a *turiya*, a shovel-like tool with a cut-out handle and a steel blade at a right angle, which had to be pushed into the earth with force. The orange trees were low, so the work had to be done in a squatting position. It was difficult and utterly exhausting.

We soon realized we would not be able to keep up this grueling work for long. After working for several hours, I had no strength left anymore. One of my companions screamed *"Dai!"* [Enough!]. We dropped our tools and walked to a clearing between the orange trees to stretch our bodies. The *ras*, the Arab foremen, were there, whips in hand, making them turn and whistle in the air, while uttering threats and insults to their crew pawns. But the moment we showed up in the clearing, they stopped. This became our work rhythm for the rest of the season: 45 minutes of intense work followed by a stretch break. The foremen never touched us or spoke to us.

As our bodies got used to the physical work, we began our social awareness mission. We tried to demonstrate to the workers through our own example that it was possible to work in a different way, to not be submissive. We also spoke to them in our imperfect Arabic. We did not speak of equality or rights, as these would be foreign terms to them; we spoke of slavery, dignity, and honor, concepts closer to their culture. For three months we worked alongside the Arab workers. They observed us and listened to us attentively without missing a detail, peering at us intently as they squatted, but they never imitated us nor stopped working. They listened, but never responded in any way.

We were tilling the same fields but lived in worlds apart. We were progressive youngsters from a European culture forging our own future; they lived in a centuries-old system based on steep class distinctions and a worldview that assigned each a destiny to live. Our words crumbled like dry leaves on the ground.

We learned that we were still far from a universal socialist dream. Over the years, as I observed the evolution of the Soviet revolution and personally visited many countries within the Soviet orbit, and through my own experience in Chile, I lost the illusion of universal socialism. It has been the great disappointment of my life.

Zemaj

There were three Arab villages in our valley, between Lake Kinneret and the town of Beisan. Two of these were farming villages; the third, Zemaj, was the home base of a band of aggressive bandits who lived on pillage, robbery, and assault. Zemaj was a strategic location, just a few meters from the electrified fence marking the boundary with Transjordan and Syria. The Hejaz Train, built by the former Ottoman empire, carried Muslim pilgrims from Turkey to Medina in Saudi Arabia, passing through Zemaj. Everybody had to cross Zemaj, whether they were traveling north-south or coming from Lebanon, Transjordan, or Syria, creating constant and intense movement of people and goods in the village.

The Zemaj bandits tricked, cheated, and robbed the pilgrims while the British guards observed unmoved; they did not intervene in "native matters." We tried to stay away from the havoc but were enraged by what happened. The bandits would place mines on the train tracks or grease the tracks to make the train slide on the slope, thus giving them time to climb onboard and assault the pilgrim passengers. When there were no pilgrims to assault, the trigger-quick bandits turned to attack our kibbutzim to steal our cattle and rape our *haverot* [female companions].

I traveled the road through Zemaj regularly to take our milk containers, filled to the brim, from our kibbutz to the communal processing plant located in the valley. It was very dangerous, so I always used our fastest horses to guide my cart. I was attacked many times by the bandits and forced to defend myself, crouching behind the metal milk containers.

A petroleum pipeline ran along the train tracks, transporting crude oil from Iraq and Syria to the refineries in the port of Haifa. To sabotage the British, the bandits perforated the pipes and ignited the oil, which then burned for days. Our apparently peaceful rural landscape was actually extremely active, especially by night: gunshots from Zemaj, burning oil, and, in the background, the howling of the jackals and the hyenas.

During Israel's War of Independence, Zemaj became a fortified center of military actions. Once the fighting was over and the armistice was signed, the bandits abandoned the village, leaving it destroyed and empty. The kibbutzim in the valley decided to erase the sour memories of the tribulations the bandits had caused, and the remnants of the town were bulldozed and flattened.

Our Arab neighbors.

ZULEIMA

BRITISH PALESTINE, 1940

Stories from *One Thousand and One Nights.*

It was a Sunday like any other. At sunrise Sigi and I opened the corral and guided our herd down the hill to cross the river to the grazing fields. At midday the animals lay down to chew the cud and rest. As I leisurely looked at the river, I noticed the water was rising abnormally. Sigi and I assessed the situation and decided to take our herd immediately back to our kibbutz. We woke up the sleepy animals with shouts and kicks and pushed the surprised animals quickly back across the river. The water had risen significantly, reaching our hips. This was not a danger for our large animals nor for us, young and strong men, and we crossed safely to the other side.

But then we spotted Zuleima, an Arab girl from the village of Abadiyah. We saw her every day taking care of her herd of goats, and we used to wave and greet each other, shouting across the fields. From her I learned my first Arabic words: good day, how are you, goodbye. I was curious about her life, but it was forbidden in her culture for her to talk to us men beyond these greetings.

We shouted to Zuleima and pointed to the river to advise her of the situation. She too decided to return and guided her little herd to the riverbank. Six of her goats crossed the river quickly and safely, but two fell into the water; she tried to pull them, but in doing so she lost her footing and fell into the water as well. Sigi and I jumped into the river, grabbed her, and took her safely out onto firm ground. Scared to death and totally wet, little Zuleima ran back to her village with her goats, screaming loud.

We recounted the event to our companions in our kibbutz communal dining room. Michael, our chief of security, listened gravely. "This is not so simple," he said. "If Zuleima tells the truth, she may be punished for losing her goats. To avoid punishment, she may say we made her fall into the water, which may trigger the ire of the elders." Michael decided not to run any risk and instructed us to be in a state of pre-emergency. He reinforced the night guard and opened our first-aid post. All was calm that night, but in the early morning our guard on the observation tower informed us: "Unusual movement in Abadiyah; a large group is gathering on the threshing square." We all waited.

From the tower, the guard reported: "Three horsemen are coming to our kibbutz." Soon we saw them emerging from the banana fields, riding magnificent horses and wearing elegant robes. As they arrived at our gate, they announced: "*Hanna al Mukhtar al Abadiyah*" [Here comes the Chief of Abadiyah], he wants to talk to the Jewish Chief." Michael stepped froward and responded: "I am the Mukhtar of this kibbutz and I welcome the Mukhtar of Abadiyah. *Merhaba!*" [Good day!]. "*Merhaba twen*" [Double good day], the Mukhtar responded, following the tradition of improving on the prior statement.

The ritual salutation dialog proceeded, each asking the other about the cows, the sheep, the goats, and the children. I asked Sigi to translate every word for me; I did not want to miss any detail of the conversation. Once the salutation was completed, the Mukhtar of Abadiyah went to the point:

"On Sunday there was an incident at the river," he said.

"Yes," responded Michael.

"An incident between two of your men and one of our girls."

"Yes."

"Never happened before around here. Two of Zuleima's goats were lost and she almost drowned in the waters."

"Yes," said Michael.

Our nerves spiked.

"If not for your men's help, she would have been dragged by the waters. I am coming to express my appreciation," said the Mukhtar.

We all breathed in relief.

The Mukhtar signaled to the two horsemen, and they presented us with a basket full of olives stuffed with spices and sweets. A delicacy! "A token of our appreciation," said the Mukhtar, and he added: "I invite your leaders to a *fantazya* in our village next Friday." And the three horsemen turned their horses and rode back to Abadiyah.

We were speechless. This had never happened before. Once we recovered, we proceeded to share the delicacies – two olives for each of our 140 *haverim*, and for Sigi and me, three.

The fantazya

Over the next few days all we talked about was the upcoming *fantazya*.

We had to decide who would attend. Our Political Committee decided that five would attend: Michael, as *Mukhtar*, Sigi and me, and two *haverim* who spoke Arabic well. It was also agreed that I needed intensive training in Arabic customs to ensure I would not embarrass anybody at the event. Our Security Committee decided that we would go unarmed but accompanied by a flare man. Our Budget Committee considered that if we wore our only good clothes, we would surely ruin them as we were inexperienced in eating with our hands, the Arab way. It was decided we would wear our work clothes, well washed. A wise decision.

On Friday evening the five of us descended the gentle slope to the river, took off our shoes to cross it, and climbed up again on the other side, to Abadiyah. From the observation tower in our kibbutz, our guard reported to our companions. From Abadiyah they were watching us as well; ten villagers walked out to meet us and took us to the village square, where they had erected poles covered with palm and banana leaves, creating a soothing shade. A strong and inviting aroma of meat and spices emanated from a large hole in the ground, covered by an enormous grill. Around the grill sat the villagers, three rows deep. The Mukhtar welcomed us and invited us to sit in the front row, each of us flanked by two of our hosts.

I showed off the Arabic I had just learned: I inquired about the children, the oxen, the cows, and the goats. I had been warned not to ask about the women. I did not ask about the fields either, as they were not the villagers' property but the *effendi's*. The animals and tools did belong to them. All this was not simple. I had to guess how many animals my host may have. If he had an ox and I asked about oxen, he might think I mocked his poverty; but if I asked about the ox, and he had several, he might think I took him for a poor man. The front of my body was sweating from the heat of the grill, but my back was sweating cold from my nerves and fear of offending my host with my limited Arabic skills. The villagers took turns to be our hosts, so six times I repeated the conversation I had mastered.

In one corner of the square were the cooks, preparing the food and surveilling the grill. In the opposite corner were the women – and I was fascinated by what I saw. The women did not participate directly in the feast. They were gathered behind a shoulder-height screen placed diagonally, and they watched the show from behind it. I could only see their heads above the screen, their faces covered by a black robe, except for their eyes. But those eyes sparkled and observed every detail, and their mouths, although covered by the black cloth, did not stop chatting for a second, commenting with humor and enthusiasm on our blue eyes, our blond hair, our poor manners, and our poor Arabic. Uncontainable laughter came from that corner, as they observed our clumsiness when eating with our hands, and the multiple mistakes in our speech. Their voices, the provocative glint in their eyes, the laughter, and the whispers left no doubt that they were having great fun and were enjoying the party as much as the men.

We shared and ate the wonderful food and the evening passed.

How does a *fantazya* end? Great Arabic wisdom: three cups of coffee are served, and after the third one, the party is over. In this way, the host can stretch time to his liking; if he enjoys your presence, he stretches the coffee service; if he has had enough, he serves the three cups one after the other. When the third cup was served and drunk, we knew it was time to leave. We bade our farewells and departed.

Back at the kibbutz, our companions asked about every detail of the party, except the menu; it was fully visible on our clothes.

The following week, Sigi and I went out to the fields again with our cattle, as usual. The goats from Abadiyah were grazing farther in the field, led by a young boy. He greeted us kindly from afar. We never saw sweet Zuleima again.

Letter in Sutterlin handwriting, 1939.

LETTERS FROM CHILE
SANTIAGO, CHILE, 1940–1942

There is no new Homeland.
Home is the land of childhood and youth.
Whoever has lost it remains lost himself.
Jean Amery, *At the Mind's Limits*

Months after my parents and sister had left Germany, I received their first letter from Chile, describing their arrival. First, my sister Hilla wrote:

My beloved brother: You may think we are in Santiago, but no – all has happened very differently from what we imagined. Our ship arrived at the port of Valparaiso on December 28, and everybody descended, except us Jewish immigrants. For two days we were forced to stay on the ship. I was very worried. But eventually, the officials allowed one person per family to descend to identify their family's luggage for customs inspection. What a chaos that was! Envision hundreds of boxes and suitcases piled haphazardly in a large courtyard. I quickly found our luggage and completed the formalities. The Chilean officials then decided to assign each family to a village or city in southern Chile. A panic broke out! Some families wanted to be with other families they knew, and everybody preferred larger cities that offered more work opportunities. Some women started to cry; the men were agitated; it was horrible. By night we still did not know our destination. Finally, it was our turn. Where to? Lautaro. The official thought it was great, but we soon learned that Lautaro is a small village where the train stops only twice a year. Rudi, amid all this uncertainty, I burst out laughing! Can you imagine being holed away with no communication? I felt myself shrivel intellectually.

At nine that night, we were instructed to take our luggage to the train. The courtyard hummed in agitation. We had to pay a bill to retrieve our luggage. The train was scheduled to depart the next morning at sunrise. The adults settled in their train seats or on the floor, as best as they could, to get some sleep overnight. We, youngsters, went for a walk. The Chilean guards shared their bread and tea with us. Finally, at six in the morning, the train departed. Rudi, the trip was very difficult; for over two full days and nights we were all crowded on the train, on hard wooden seats or on the floor, lacking ventilation and without any food or water.

While on the train, we were able to change our destination to Valdivia instead of Lautaro. We heard that Valdivia is a cultured and beautiful city, and we would be with other immigrants assigned there. That afternoon, the train stopped in Lautaro. Rudi, there is no way I would have stayed there. There is barely a paved street, people are dressed in rags, all kinds of activities take place on the streets, and there is not one immigrant in town. One hour later we arrived in Temuco, which is, for local standards, a large city with 34,000 inhabitants. Half of the passengers descended there.

Now, this was December 31st, New Year's Eve. The train was scheduled to stay in Temuco for several hours, and to leave at two in the morning of the new year. So, I joined a group of youngsters to go visit the city along with some men from the local Jewish Committee and the train conductor. They took us to a restaurant. I had to be polite and drank three glasses of vermouth which made me feel tipsy. Just before two in the morning we returned to the train, but the departure had been delayed to three o'clock. We left again and ended up at a large dancing hall, where dressed-up people were celebrating the new year, 1940. A nice gentleman offered to pay our entry fee and even bought us some soda drinks. At three in the morning, we returned to the train, but it was delayed again. I spent the time chatting with a carabinero – this is how a policeman is called here – in the best Spanish that I could muster. He gave me a note with his address and indicated that he was not engaged and would soon travel to Valdivia!

We finally arrived in Valdivia at mid-day of January 1st. We were taken to the local Jewish Committee – Central Israelita Doctor Herzl – in a gondola, which is the local bus. We had no place to stay and no money. A local Jewish lady invited me to lodge at her home for a few days, while Vati looked for a place to stay. The nice lady bought me ice cream. But Rudi, here in Valdivia there are many Germans, and the newspapers have written horrible things about us Jewish immigrants, all lies and falsehoods.

But I trust all will be better eventually. I hope we can later move to Santiago, as Valdivia is just a large village. But most important and wonderful is that we are out of Germany. Jews are having a very, very difficult time there, banned from jobs and schools, forced to wear an armband with a yellow star... We are extremely worried about Onkel Fritz and our friends. You will soon receive more letters from us. Much love from your Hilla.

My father added:

Dear son: Here we are, in Valdivia. Everything is quite different from what we imagined. If this is what must be, then so be it. Hilla described to you the train trip, which was extremely difficult for us. We had no money, no food, no water, and could not leave the crowded train for three long days and nights. I was not in a mood to celebrate the new year. My mind was focused on how to provide for us all. The climate here is quite agreeable. If I can find some work, this may be a place where we can live.

Where are you, dearest son? Eight weeks without news from you, not one line. Our address is for now: "Chile, Valdivia, Poste Restante." Stay healthy, my son. Your Vati.

A few months later I received another letter; Vati, Mutti, and Hilla wrote tightly on the same sheet of paper to save space and postage costs. First, my mother:

My beloved, good son: We finally got news from you! This is first letter we receive from you since we left Germany. We are delighted to know that you are alive. We are slowly getting used to this new place. Compared to European standards, this is very different. We must readjust our mindset on living conditions, hygiene, and punctuality. Fleas, flies, and insects are now part of our daily life. It is very difficult to get housing, so we are still living in a modest guesthouse. Vati is looking into a possible job representing a powder custard product. As for Vati's profession as a chemist-pharmacist, it seems quite impossible to find work in that capacity. Hilla will start to work next week as a housekeeper with a local family. I hope our girl will be well. As you can see, the good God does not abandon us. A thousand kisses, from your Mutti.

My father's addition followed:

My dear son: I hope the powder custard product representation works out. I must earn money to support us. Compared to Germany, everything is cheaper here, but salaries are much lower as well. The local currency is the peso. One German Mark is equivalent to 30 pesos. Living conditions and lifestyle are completely different from what we are used to. Living conditions are quite primitive, although the city has nearly 40,000 residents. We must adjust completely our standards for wellbeing, cleanliness, manners, punctuality, and eating. And everybody is here so slow! The most frequently used word is mañana *– which means "tomorrow," but really means to say, "not now, maybe at some unknown future time." Everything will be done "mañana." Businesses close at mid-day between twelve and two, and everybody goes home to eat and sleep. People eat only white bread; the black bread we are used to eat is nowhere to be found. I miss the Käsestulles, made of dark bread with a thick slice of cheese that Mutti used to prepare for us in Berlin. When will we see you again, dear son? Regards from your Vati.*

And lastly my sister Hilla:

Dear brother: I start working on March 1st. This will provide us with some money, and ease my parents' worry a bit. When we first arrived in Valdivia, I thought I would never get used to this city, but as time goes by, I am starting to like it more. I have become friends with a girl I met on the ship. In the evenings, we go for a walk around the main square, where everybody gathers, and we are known as two exotic birds. I find Chileans to be two-faced. A boy may talk to us and go out for a walk one day, and then the next day, he behaves as if we had never met. My friend and I do not care much, as we have no expectations, so the boys approach us more than the other girls. We get horrible news from Germany. What will happen to Onkel Fritz and our Oma? We cannot help them from here; it is impossible to get a visa to Chile.

Immigration was difficult. My father was over 60 and not at all prepared to learn a new language and start a new life in such a different culture. He was a seasoned and respected chemist-pharmacist in Berlin, but he could not get a job in Valdivia. The owner of the largest pharmacy said to him, "A qualified pharmacist like you, I will never find in this city; however, if I employ you, I will lose my clients, because you are a Jew."

My mother's severe arthritis limited her mobility, and Valdivia's humid climate worsened her ailment. Their financial situation was extremely difficult. Hilla, 14 years old, became head of household, solving problems, translating for her parents, and working several jobs to support them. At her first job, as live-in domestic help for a local family, she slept on a roll-out mattress on the kitchen floor.

After several months, Hilla decided to move the family to Santiago, the capital, for better work opportunities.

Dear son: We received your letter dated September. We were delighted to receive news from you. We get only bad news from Berlin. I am now working at the Berger Pharmacy in Santiago. Pharmaceutical practices are here quite different compared to Germany. Here, pharmacies take a commercial approach, rather than scientific; they are essentially

The family's initial years in Santiago were challenging. They rented a room in a boardinghouse, along with other Jewish and Spanish immigrant families. Fourteen people lived in the house, sharing one kitchen and one bathroom. For two years, the one room was their home. Hilla had to share a bed with her mother and did not go to school, as she had to work to help support the family. Initially she worked two jobs, a day job and a night job, until she was able to get a better job in a bookstore. She then joined a Jewish youth group, which provided a rich social and intellectual circle that nurtured her and helped her face the daily challenges. My father worked ten hours a day for a minimal salary. My mother's health deteriorated, and they lived with the constant concern over the destiny of friends and family trapped in Germany and their anguish for me on the war front.

My parents and sister continued writing regularly, sending me their love across the ocean, but they never fully described their challenges, their financial hardships, their poor living conditions, the miserable work, and their anxiety for those still trapped in Germany. They tried to send me good news, to ease my worry for them. They were safe; that was all that mattered.

My letters to them from the kibbutz were also half-truths. I described the warm reception the kibbutz elders gave us, but not our harsh living conditions. I described the wheat and alfalfa fields, but not the open blisters on my hands. I described the banana harvest, but not the backache, nor that I broke down from exhaustion and pain. I did not describe our self-defense training or the nights in the bunker guarding our settlement from attacks.

What for? It would only increase their worry. No, I wanted them to trust that I was safe on the other side of the globe.

Thus, the letters in both directions were just signs of survival.

IN THE HAGANAH
BRITISH PALESTINE, 1941

He that keepeth Israel
shall neither slumber nor sleep.
Psalms 121:4

A large tract of land near Zemaj had been put up for sale by its owner, an Arab *effendi*. Although the land was not cultivated, had limited access, and was in a dangerous area, the Jewish National Fund acquired it to expand farming production and establish a new kibbutz. Since the area was prone to ambushes, for the foundation of the new kibbutz we applied the technique of *Homa u'migdal* [stockade and tower], based on surprise and rapid action.

All the kibbutzim in the valley participated in the preparations. We prefabricated all the key buildings, the water tank, the observation tower, the defense palisades, and procured an electric generator, machinery, and tools. On the designated day for the foundation, we rose before dawn and moved to the new kibbutz site to help construct the encampment. I was very proud of my responsibility: to drive a large platform car loaded with large tools, part of a caravan carrying all the materials we had prepared.

On arrival, a group of youngsters started to build the fence and the observation tower; another group built the sheds for the machinery and the seeds; a third group set up the tents for the pioneers of the new kibbutz to sleep in. At midday, two tractors started to plow the land. By nightfall, the new kibbutz was fully established and functioning. The volunteers retreated to their homes and the founding *haverim* of the new kibbutz went to rest in their tents to gather strength for the next workday. The guards sat on the observation tower to scan for any night dangers.

The southern portion of the new land was not safe enough to establish a kibbutz. Instead, we opted to farm these lands communally. The most critical periods were the harvest and the threshing season. We all arrived from our kibbutzim with our tractors, our cutters, our threshers, and our balers – an agricultural army. We worked non-stop from sunrise to sunset. Our trucks and carts drove in with supplies and then drove out with the baled wheat all day long. At dusk we formed a defensive ring with our machinery and tractors around our campsite with our tents and camp kitchen, and we rested. The designated guards settled behind the bales of straw, on the tractors, or under the trailers.

We were frequently attacked during the harvests; we always resisted the onslaught. We shot back, trying not to kill. No one wanted to kill, not even in self-defense. We just wanted to drive the attackers away, discourage them. We did not want to provoke or provide reasons for revenge. We always gave the attackers an opportunity to evacuate their wounded. We resisted many attacks in those years, but we never found a dead body outside our palisades the next morning.

These confrontations were my baptism of fire. I learned defense tactics and learned the military philosophy that would guide me in the coming years, which I did not even suspect at that time.

To Lebanon

The security of our kibbutzim was a constant challenge. We had to protect our workers in the field and defend ourselves from nightly attacks; we had to buy weapons, learn to use them, and develop tactics. Our self-defense was successful, but it was extremely time consuming and a huge financial drain.

A British officer sympathetic to our cause, Captain Orde Wingate, initiated in 1938 the creation of new joint British–Jewish field units that operated beyond the kibbutzim defenses to face the terrorists in the open field. I was assigned to one of these field units.

Under Wingate's initiative and led by Moshe Dayan, the emerging military genius who would later lead the Israeli Army during the Six Day War in 1967, these units proved very successful. Eventually, these units became the Palmach strike forces and were later incorporated into the Haganah, the Jewish self-defense organization in British-ruled Palestine.

When the German Army advanced into North Africa and became a real and immediate threat in 1940, the British Army and the Haganah agreed to collaborate in joint defense actions. The initial goal was to prevent a German landing in Lebanon, a country controlled by the French Vichy government, sympathizer with Nazi Germany. The first planned action was to sabotage the oil installations in Lebanon to impede the provision of fuel to German aircraft and thus thwart the German invasion of Lebanon and Syria. The Palmach field units' experience was crucial to guide the British troops through the complex terrain towards their target. Moshe Dayan directed the scouting operation.

He organized two groups. One commando group set out along the coast in rubber boats to take position from behind. The boats never made it to their destination, and 23 young men were lost at sea. This was a terrible blow to our tight community, in which each life was treasured. The second group, composed of a mix of British troops and Palmach men, departed from Metullah, just south of the Lebanese border, to Jiam El Valid, the first Lebanese French bastion. Twenty highly qualified men were selected for this operation, but Dayan decided to include 30 additional men as trainees. I was part of this trainee group; my first large-scale action.

The operation lasted 30 hours and was a success. Dayan's unit crossed the border, secured two bridges over the Litani River and captured the Vichy police station. We were exhausted and preparing to rest when we were suddenly bombarded by artillery. We all threw ourselves to the ground – all except Dayan and his lieutenant, who climbed onto a rooftop to examine the situation. A shell exploded next to them and the splinters broke Dayan's binoculars and penetrated his eye. He lost an eye, and from then on wore the black patch which, along with his military genius, made him famous.

These joint military operations cemented a strong collaboration between the British Army and the Haganah. Months later, when the German Army advanced into Egypt, and the British Army urgently needed to increase its ranks with experienced soldiers, the members of the Haganah volunteered en masse to join the British Army.

And so did I.

Me, soldier of the British Army, 3rd Infantry Battalion, Palestine
Regiment.

THE JEWISH BRIGADE
BRITISH PALESTINE, 1942–1946

Serving Member of His Majesty's Forces.
Profession listed in my British-Palestinian passport

The war was the main topic of all our conversations at the kibbutz. The German Army was advancing from one victory to the next, and we dreaded what this meant for our families and for the Jews of Europe. We listened to horrible news on our radio in the communal dining room. On the wall above the radio, we hung a map of Europe on which we marked the war's development. The pins showed the German Army penetrating deeper and deeper into Eastern Europe.

And then, in 1941, the German Afrika Korps landed in North Africa.

The British Army was ill prepared for this offensive. The German Afrika Korps, led by General Rommel, advanced across Libya to the Egyptian frontier – our own backyard. The British fought heroically with reinforcement troops drafted from Australia and New Zealand, but it lost all battles. The German and Italian units under Rommel's command, advanced into Egypt, menacing the British control of the Suez Canal and with it, the whole Middle East oil resources. The German invasion of British Palestine was imminent, and the British Army was considering a scenario for withdrawal to Syria or Iraq. This would be a disaster for the British and even a worse one for our Jewish community. The situation was desperate.

The British defeats were caused, in the first place, by the poor tactics of the military high command in Africa, and secondly, by the reduced number of troops because of men lost in battle and the need to attend to multiple war fronts in Europe. At that crucial moment, Winston Churchill, the British prime minister, made two fundamental decisions. He appointed a new commander to the British Eighth Army in North Africa: General Bernard Montgomery, a man who inspired the confidence to face the military genius of Rommel. Churchill also decided to reinforce the troops in Africa, calling for men from the nearby sources: South Africa and the Jews of Palestine.

We understood very clearly that the war in Africa was about our own Jewish survival. The Sokhnut – the Jewish Agency of Israel in British Palestine – offered to call Jewish volunteers to join the British Army under two conditions: first, that the volunteers would serve in their own "Palestine Regiment"; and second, that half of the volunteers would be deployed specifically to defend Palestine. The Sokhnut would not risk that all Jewish volunteers could lose their lives in North Africa and leave their own community in Palestine deprived of its youth to defend it from a German invasion. The British accepted the conditions.

Calling for volunteers was a daily practice within our Jewish community, but the response to the call to serve in the British Army surpassed all expectations: 25,000 young men and 3,000 young women raised their arms and volunteered, and I was among them.

The British were thrilled, not only because of the large number of volunteers but because most of them had prior military training from defending our kibbutzim. There was little the British had to teach us beyond military formalities and greetings. And thus, in early 1942, the Palestine Regiment was formed.

I was fully immersed in the formation of our kibbutz at that time; but I realized that history was being shaped in Africa at that crucial moment. I joined the Third Infantry Battalion of the new Palestine Regiment, platoon 775. This would be my new identity for the next four years: PAL 38691.

The Jewish people were going through their greatest challenge. European Jewry was endangered to its core and – without us fully knowing it yet – in the throes of annihilation. Who would form the thread of continuity of Jewish identity? There was no time for speeches or philosophy, but we intuitively knew we had to take on this role and act on it. There were one million Jewish soldiers in the Allied armies, fighting as either English, Americans, French, or Russians. Now, we would fight in our own Jewish unit, with our own badges and our own flag. We were ready for this historic challenge.

The British Army deployed us into special units designated to resist the expected German invasion of British Palestine. We were preparing for a second Massada, the heroic Jewish stronghold against the Romans in the year A.D.132. As part of this strategy, 90 of us who had a German background were trained to form a new intelligence unit, the *Pluga Germanit* [German unit]. We were given German soldiers' uniforms and learned to impersonate a German *Landser* [soldier], with the goal of infiltrating the German lines when they arrived in our territory. I was barely 20 years old and was eager to immerse myself in this mission.

And then, in October of 1942, the great battle of El Alamein took place. El Alamein was a small town strategically located in the Egyptian desert, near the Suez Canal. It was the last chance to stop the inexorable advance of the German Afrika Korps under Rommel's lead. The British Eighth Army, now reorganized and reinforced with men from Australia, India, New Zealand, South Africa, and our Palestinian soldiers, totaling 220,000 men, under the command of General Montgomery, won this decisive battle.

Montgomery envisioned the battle as an attrition operation and ensured superb Allied air support, which had a huge effect on the battle. The Germans were forced to retreat into Tunisia, and with that, the greatest and immediate danger to our Jewish community in British Palestine was over. All of us soldiers who had prepared to face the German invasion in Palestine were immediately moved to Egypt, where we joined the British combatant units on the Africa campaign. We kept to our tactics: we never lost contact with the enemy, we stuck to their heels, gave them no respite or time to reorganize. We pressed through Algeria and Tunisia, taking the port of Tripoli in January of 1943. With much effort, we finally defeated the German Afrika Korps in May of 1943. This tough and long Africa campaign lasted seven months.

The battle of El Alamein coincided with the Allied invasion of French North Africa and the Battle of Stalingrad, and these three crucial victories revived the morale of the Allies in this very long war. "Before Alamein we never had a victory. After Alamein we never had a defeat," said Churchill.

At the end of the Africa campaign our Palestine Regiment was renamed the "Jewish Brigade." We now proudly wore our own badges and insignias with the Star of David on a light blue background.

Ferocity

"Heroism," "good soldier," and "sacrifice," were terms we used daily during the war. There was no time to ponder or philosophize, but the intense war actions and fighting experiences certainly shaped our values. I witnessed over and over how some men always ran ahead in battle, while others remained slightly behind. In wartime, people are classified based on their courage, initiative, and determination. I reflected on the words of my high school philosophy teacher: the one who risks more is not necessarily more heroic. Bravery is the capacity to perform properly even when scared to death. A fearful one who achieves the goal is perhaps more courageous because of the greater fear he had to overcome. I tried to keep this in mind before judging my companion unit members.

War distorts our values. In war, people are valued mostly for their military qualities. For this reason, there was contempt towards the Italian soldiers, who were not considered as brave as the

German or the British; and German soldiers were clearly more ferocious than the British. Ferocity may not be a value in civilian life, but in times of war, it was clearly a plus. Our commander decided to teach us ferocity to overcome our disadvantage.

We began with bayonet exercises. We did not fight with bayonets in actual battle, but our commander thought it was a good tool to teach us ferocity. Our squad was divided into two groups, each facing the other in an open field. We were ordered to run at each other with our bayonets. We initially assumed a formation with a reasonable distance between ourselves and those on our right and left, and then at each round, at tighter and tighter distances. Instinctively we tended to slow down as we ran at each other this way, to aim for the small gap between bodies with our bayonets. We did not really want to skewer our own companions. Our officer exploded in rage.

He prepared a new exercise, hanging big sacks from a horizontal bar. We were to run at the bag, dig in the bayonet with all our strength, raise a knee, jam the bag, take the bayonet out, and then repeat with another "victim". We had done this exercise before with straw-filled sacks, so we ran confidently towards the hanging bags, smiling slightly. But this time the sacks were filled with live cats. With our bayonets we nailed the sacks, the cats shrieked, and the sacks gushed blood as we kept digging the bayonets again and again, until there were no more shrieks. Large pools of blood formed on the ground. Then we had to pick up the bags, leave the dead bodies on the ground and finish off those who still showed signs of life.

There were no more small smiles, only deadly silence.

British Intelligence Corps, Cairo, 1943. I am in the center
in the back row.

Prisoners waiting in line for their food rations, North
Africa, 1942.

AGENT OF THE INTELLIGENCE SERVICE
SUEZ, AFRICA, 1943

Here you will be witnesses to history.
Colonel Roberts, British Army, Africa campaign

Fresh winds were blowing in the British Army. After suffering defeat after defeat, the British Army won the decisive battle in El Alamein and turned into a victorious army. The fresh winds also reached our Jewish Brigade. British intelligence officers approached our unit for volunteers for military intelligence work. A thousand of us volunteered and 120 of us were selected.

We were offered three specialties for further training. Many of us chose the Commandos: elite units of men that spoke perfect German and looked perfectly German, who would be dressed in German uniforms and placed behind the Afrika Korps lines, with a single purpose: to capture Rommel. The training was extremely rigorous: we had to walk for eight hours through the desert, execute a mission and return the same way. I failed this very demanding endurance test. The Commando Unit was formed with the very best 15 men, but they never accomplished their ultimate mission.

The second specialty also seemed very exciting: spies. I passed the initial selection and was assigned a practice test, along with four other trainees. The British Army had initiated a campaign to re-educate the German prisoners held in camps along the Suez Canal, by imparting history, ethics, and English lessons. Success was particularly low in camps #180 and #182, where Nazi prisoner leaders did not allow their fellow prisoners to participate in the lessons. During the night they killed those who chose re-education, strangling them with their blankets. This would be the scenario for our practice test.

Suez

Our mission was to impersonate a German soldier and enter camps #180 and #182 to discover the Nazi ringleaders within five days. I applied everything I had learned to prepare myself thoroughly. I identified a German soldier whom I would impersonate. He was a young man about my age who had grown up in the Moabit district in Berlin, which I knew well because my grandparents had lived there. I interrogated him intensely for two days, posing as a reporter and offering him beer, cigarettes, and other temptations to make him talk. I made him describe his personal story, read his personal letters, and detail the ups and downs of his battalion before and during the Africa campaign. I made him repeat some details over and over, to learn them to perfection. I was able to penetrate the man's personality and his unit mentality. Two days later I sent him back to his camp, after stripping him of his uniform, including his underwear and his war amulets. I then dressed in his sweaty clothes and placed his documents, photos, and two letters in the pockets of his clothes. Not only did I have to look like a German soldier, I also had to smell like one. I was ready.

There I was, at six in the morning, waiting for the British Army truck that would take me to prisoners' camp #182 on the banks of the Suez Canal. I took one last look in a mirror at my image of a *Landser*, a rifleman of Rommel's Africa Korps. I could smell the odor of the desert sand-soaked uniform, sweaty and unwashed. I took a deep breath; my five days of action were about to begin.

Our British commander simulated a prisoners' swap, taking 200 prisoners out of camps #180 and #182 and introducing 200 new ones, with us five spy trainees among them. We were given a password to use in case of emergency. I crossed the barbed wire into camp #182. A German sergeant assigned me a bunkbed in one of the tented barracks and explained the camp's regulations. "Your bunkbed is number 236 in barrack C, under my command," he said. The barrack smelled intensely – 420 soldiers living in compact space – but my bunkbed 236 had a particularly horrible odor. I sighed and left my backpack there, with my documents and the two letters.

I tried to contain my nervousness. I chatted with other prisoners to test my impersonation. I responded to their questions about my war experience, and – as a newcomer – shared with them some news about the development of the war. I watched carefully in case anything in my use of language or behavior triggered any unusual questions. It seemed I was doing a good job. I inquired about the camp's activities and about the peculiar odor of my bunkbed. My fellow prisoners looked at me sideways and lowered their voices to a hush. "The man who slept in your bunkbed was executed a couple nights ago for being a dissident. The camp's commando unit strangled him with his blanket, and he vomited as he died. That's what you are smelling." I swallowed, took a silent breath, and hid my horror.

I began to investigate. I asked around carefully and quickly learned that the brain of the Nazi camp ring was in the infirmary. The next day I showed up there complaining of a migraine, to seek out more information. I would have to speed up to meet my goal. There was much information still missing and I only had two days left.

The next morning, we lined up for the daily roll call. One prisoner was missing. The British sergeant sent a guard to check the barracks. The missing man had been strangled in his bunkbed; it was one of my British companions.

I decided to keep a low profile for the rest of the day. For the first time I felt acute, intense fear. Maybe the ringleaders had already discovered that I was an impostor, a spy; maybe they were preparing their vengeance, forming the commando for that night.

How could I have been so naïve as to believe in the movies, in which spies walk around in silk shirts and sleep confidently at night?

As soldiers, we knew that death could be our destiny. We tried to ignore it, not to think about it, but even when we thought about death, we imagined it would happen in battle, while fighting. No, I did not want to die strangled with my blanket in the anonymity of a prisoners' camp, dressed like a German soldier. I decided to sleep during the day, to stay awake during the night and be prepared for what might happen.

Summer nights in the African desert are short. But this night seemed endless to me. Any sound, any noise, seemed suspicious. The snoring of the men in the bunkbeds above and below me: maybe they were pretending, waiting for me to fall asleep. Or maybe it was those who were not snoring that were waiting for me to fall asleep to jump on me. I heard the soft noise of feet on the sandy floor, barely audible. Terror invaded me – they are coming for me! But no, these were just the steps of one man going to the bathroom. I then heard soft steps coming from the opposite direction. There was no bathroom there – they are coming for me now! But no, the man shuffled past my bunkbed to lay with his partner. Oh, that night was endless, endless.

Finally, the first rays of light poured in through the thick fabric of our tent. The new day was breaking, and I was still alive. My clothes now had a new ingredient mixed with the desert sweat: the cold sweat of fear, of terror.

That day, to my surprise and relief, one of my companions called his password and all of us trainees were immediately taken out of the prisoners' camp. My companion had identified the Nazi ringleaders and completed the mission successfully.

I realized I did not have what it takes to be a spy.

The runner

I was then selected to join a new unit, the Combined Services Detailed Interrogation Corps (CSDIC), as a frontline interrogator.

Our role was to advance with the frontline troops and interrogate the German and Italian prisoners on the spot, at the front. Our goal was to obtain as much military and tactical information as possible while the soldier was seized by fear and confusion at the moment of his capture. This information was then delivered to our frontline commanders to help them make better tactical decisions and improve their position for combat. The creation of our unit was a great success from the start, as we obtained crucial information that saved the lives of many of our soldiers.

Our success pushed for the growth of our unit, and new men joined us: Kemeny, a Jewish refugee from Budapest, came from the Australian battalion; Spira, a Jew from Vienna, came from the New Zealander battalion; Fekete, originally from Hungary, came from the South African battalion; from the French Foreign Legion came Weil, a Jew from Saarbrücken; and from India came Levin with his turban. A wild mix of nationalities and characters.

One day, I was called urgently by our Advanced Field Hospital. If you want to smell the pain of war, go to a field hospital. It is a torment for those lying on stretchers scattered on the sand, helpless, writhing in pain, and waiting for their turn for surgery. And it is a torment also for those who attend to them. The wounded grab your leg and beg for water, or for cool bandages for their wounds, but they also beg you: "Sarge, please be my friend, finish me off."

The doctor on duty took me to a stretcher in the post-surgery section. A British officer lay there sleeping. An exploding mine had shattered his leg, which had just been amputated. The doctor had applied anesthesia and instructed the soldier to count, to ensure he was indeed asleep before proceeding with the surgery. The soldier had begun to count: "One, two, three, four, *fünf, sechs, sieben, acht,*" going from English to German as he fell asleep. "I think this case is for you," the doctor said.

I checked the soldier's military documents. They looked legitimate and in perfect order. I searched the man's small battle bag, which contained the usual items a soldier carried. But something was missing: personal items. When going to battle, we store our personal items in a very small side pocket. We are loaded with ammunition and weapons, carrying excess weight, and have little space for anything else. But every soldier masters the art of packing his most personal items in that minimal space. No soldier goes to fight without carrying a personal object along with his documents in that small pocket specially prepared to withstand weather. The personal object symbolizes "his own" war – a letter from his girlfriend or his children, a picture of his parents, a ring, even a small stone. No soldier fights without this. It's your amulet. But this man's bag contained no amulet at all.

I ripped the bag apart and, alas, I found a miniature pocket, two centimeters wide, hidden in a double bottom and holding 15 small pieces of paper with confidential military information. One paper listed our units in a specific section of the front. Another was a diagram of a pillbox, an ingenious portable bunker that the British Army had developed. A third one showed the supply lines to our front.

I climbed on my motorcycle with the man's bag and rushed to our headquarters in Cairo. Hurried, perspired, and agitated, I stood in front of my colonel. He looked at me and said, "Sergeant, you are exhausted and dirty. Go take a shower and then come back to explain your thoughts." Half an hour later I was back; my colonel and his senior intelligence officers had already studied the documents and ascertained that the injured man was a "runner," responsible for transferring military information to the German front.

With the capture of the runner, we penetrated a German espionage network that was operating behind our lines. Our experts observed that the runner's information was very specific and therefore was sourced not from within the troops but from some higher level. Who could be committing this treason? Our officers concluded that it was coming from within the Egyptian Army. The Egyptian Army was officially a British ally, but the Egyptians really hated the British who occupied their land, They yearned for a German victory, in the hope that this would liberate them from the British yoke, and so they lent themselves to espionage in favor of the Germans.

We identified that the spy cell was within the Egyptian supply and transport unit serving the British troops. A military raid was organized, and the key Egyptian officers were arrested for interrogation. I remember well the words of our captain: "Young men, you are true witnesses of history." I was only 21 and was struck by this image and responsibility. At that moment I decided to keep a war diary, and on my next day off in Cairo, I bought a notebook. For the next three years I wrote regularly in my diary recording my experiences.

By then I had already learned three keys of good intelligence work: first, thoroughness and accuracy in obtaining and manipulating information; second, patience, which is the hardest to learn; and third, good luck. Here I was, a rookie without any merit, and luck had smiled on me, involving me in a unique espionage case.

We formed teams to cross-examine the Egyptian officers and were given precise instructions on how to proceed. My soulmate Bobby and I formed a team and were assigned four men for questioning. Our first task was to write down their names; the Arabic names were difficult to pronounce and even more difficult to write in English spelling. One of the men we were assigned was called Anwar Sadat, a name that meant nothing to us at that moment. We questioned him like all others, and he was kept under arrest for the rest of the war. After the war, Anwar Sadat formed part of the "Free Officers" who overthrew Egypt's King Farouk in 1952 and installed themselves to rule Egypt under the leadership of Gamal Abdel Nasser. Twenty-five years later, in 1970, Anwar Sadat became president of Egypt, and ten years later, in 1979, he offered peace to Israel and made the historic trip from Cairo to Jerusalem, where a peace was signed between the two nations that is still in place today. In 1970, my friend Bobby wrote to me: "Rudi, do you remember we questioned him in 1943?" Bobby, who is much bolder than I, sent a letter to Sadat: "Mr. Sadat, do you recall year 1943 when you were taken prisoner and interrogated by two sergeants? I was one of them." And Sadat replied: "Of course I remember!" and invited Bobby for a banquet at his presidential palace. Two years later Sadat was murdered by some of his own people who considered him a traitor for having made peace with Israel.

Indeed, we were witnesses to history; and history forms unpredictable circles in time.

In search of the radar

Our unit headquarters were in Maadi, the most elegant suburb in Cairo. The big bosses wanted to live comfortably, and in this dry and hot country, Maadi was a true oasis, the place we all loved to return to after periods of intense field work. In Maadi the streets were paved and lined with large, leafy trees that provided a soothing shade. Our offices were comfortable, and we ate well, complementing the tasteless military food with wonderful ingredients from Cairo's markets: falafel, lentils, chickpeas; lamb meat, onions, spices, and delicious phyllo sweets.

In our Maadi headquarters functioned a sophisticated British intelligence center. High-ranking German and Italian prisoners were sent to Maadi for interrogation and housed in rooms in pairs of two men unknown to each other. The high-ranking prisoners were welcomed with handshakes in sumptuous salons with soft chairs, drinks, and cigarettes, to put them at ease, soften them, and incite them to release valuable data. An informant that is at ease needs guidance rather than interrogation. These were the very early days of intelligence technology, and magnetic recording devices did not yet exist. The British Army introduced a new method to collect information: microphones were installed hidden inside the ceiling lamps in the prisoners' rooms. Once the prisoners returned to their rooms after the interrogations in the sumptuous salons, we sat in a separate room and listened in to their conversations with their room partners, with whom they would share what they had said or not said. Some preferred to talk at night only, assuming the guards might be spying on them, but we had German and Italian-speaking agents listening 24 hours a day.

This provided us with a unique insight into German thoughts, intentions, and capabilities. We obtained excellent information which we then analyzed, organized, and sent to the corresponding army, navy, or aviation unit.

We were chosen for this intelligence work because of our German background and our mastery of the German language and culture. We learned the details of the German military, including the uniforms, badges, medals, weapons, machinery, and vehicles used by each unit. With this knowledge we could better understand the prisoners' mentality and what they were talking about. We were instrumental in building their confidence and making them more willing to talk to us in direct interrogations. We were strictly forbidden to do anything forceful, and we were more successful at our job because of it. It was fascinating work because we discovered many new leads.

Among the prisoners was a German electrical engineer who had created the first radar to be placed in the Libyan desert. I interrogated him jointly with a Royal Airforce officer. The German engineer was willing to talk to us and agreed to guide us to the remote location where the radar equipment had been abandoned. He was not a fanatical Nazi nor an anti-Nazi. He was, above all, passionate about technology and scientific progress, and he loathed to think that his radar, which he had built with so much effort, ingenuity, and passion, would be lost simply because of the withdrawal of the German Army. He wanted to save his radar at all costs.

We organized an expedition to look for the radar. A mechanic-driver, the Air Force officer, the German engineer, and I, as leader and interpreter, formed the group. We prepared a jeep with a trailer and supplies for four days and set out into the desert, following the engineer's directions. We traveled for a whole day, set up camp, and started the search. For two days we searched tirelessly in the desert but, to everyone's great disappointment, we never found the radar. I directed one extra day of search, to no avail. On the fourth day, before sunrise, we started on our way back. In the desert, visibility is best at daybreak, before the onset of heat, which creates air movement and distorts the view.

The war in Africa was fought on two fronts: the German enemy and the hostile environment. We had to survive on only two liters of water per day for drinking, washing, shaving, and refreshing; we had to eat always with our back to the wind, no matter how gentle, otherwise we ate sand; our hair turned into dry wire and broke painfully when touched; and worst of all, it was very, very easy to get lost in the desert forever.

And so here we were, carefully tracking our way back, searching the landscape with our powerful binoculars to find our way, when suddenly, the German prisoner pointed out to the far side. The Air Force officer scanned the distant horizon with his binoculars: "There is an undefined black spot; no, two; they seem to move; yes, definitely moving points." We drove our jeep towards the moving points, stopping every few minutes to let the sand cloud caused by our vehicle to settle down. As we got closer, we realized that the two points were two people. There was no radar, but here were two German soldiers, lost in the desert for days, nearly dead for lack of water. A third had died some days before. The agonizing German soldiers, my hated enemies, were begging the British for mercy. I felt anger. We had not organized this expedition and exhausted our resources to save the lives of German soldiers. But I could not leave them abandoned in the desert. We were combatants, not murderers. We gave them water and loaded them onto our trailer intended to carry the big radar.

For a long time, I considered the frustrated radar search with anger. Only years later did I come to understand that it was an important experience to realize that our humanism, either innate or acquired through tradition and education, is part of our core being.

The radar was never found.

AL-QAHIRA
AFRICA 1942–1943

I will give you the good of the land of Egypt
and ye shall eat the fat of the land.
Genesis 45:18

Al-Qahira – Cairo – was an oasis, a flash of civilization, a most desired heaven. It was every soldier's dream to spend a few days, and hopefully many, in the big city of Cairo. Having our intelligence unit headquarters in the best of Cairo's neighborhoods was a great privilege. But Cairo had many faces: work Cairo, party Cairo, Jewish Cairo, cultural Cairo.

There was much culture to enjoy in Cairo, but it was completely ignored by most soldiers. These were harsh war times and life hung by a thread. Death and destruction, letters from anguished relatives, and our own youth, were not conducive to matters of culture. I visited the pyramids and the city's renowned Egyptian Museum, where only a handful of soldiers looked at the displays. What I enjoyed most of cultural Cairo was a British institution called "Music for All," which provided music concerts for the troops in an old cinema on Marouf Street, which had been adapted with a piano and a gramophone. The program included recorded concerts, visiting artists, and the Cairo Orchestra. The modern music events were always full of soldiers who never tired of listening to the tunes in vogue: "Begin the Begin," "Smoke Gets in Your Eyes," or Frank Sinatra's "Strangers in the Night." I also enjoyed the smaller but well-attended classical music events, with their pleasant and cultured atmosphere.

Al-Qahira Al-Fantazya [Party Cairo]

Party Cairo was the most desired, the busiest face of the city. More than a million soldiers – British, Australians, Palestinian Jews, New Zealanders, South Africans, Foreign Legion, French, Bengalis, and others who were part of the British Eighth Army in North Africa, turned to Cairo's entertainment on their free days to escape the war front. Drinks, shows, singing, bodily pleasures, and total debauchery. "To have a hell of a good time" was the maxim.

The Egyptian businessmen knew their trade: you name it, they had it. The preferred activity was getting drunk to unconsciousness. Beers were sold per square meter, and after a few hours, the empty bottles were on the tables and the soldiers on the floor. The stench of alcohol mixed with urine and vomit is etched in my memory. Many times, those of us who did not drink had to drag our drunken companions out of the nightclubs and back to the barracks to sign them in on time.

For those looking for entertainment, there were shows everywhere: belly dancing or the "dance of the seven veils", staged in enormous halls seating 300 to 500 soldiers on bleachers with tables to hold beer and whiskey, surrounding a central stage. The air was so dense that it could be cut with a bayonet. Women with gigantic balloon-like breasts circulated between the tables with a bag tied to their breasts to collect money. The men placed one Egyptian pound into this bag, reaching deep down with their hand and even their forearm between the women's breasts, and feel the erotic pleasure of the warm, soft flesh, the perspiration, and her false sighs. When all dues had been collected, the women began their dance on stage. The dance created a great buzz; the soldiers shouted, cajoling the women to go from veil to veil, to no veil at all.

In playful Cairo there was also room for clean-cut young men like me: there was Suleiman Pasha Avenue, the most elegant street in Cairo, with a lush tree canopy and lined with stately four-story buildings in Cairo's wonderful architectural style, combining French neoclassicism with Levantine ornamentation. The most fashionable stores and elegant cafes were there. Everything was offered: clothes, jewelry, perfumes, leather, watches, the imaginable and the unimaginable. It was for me a world of illusion, a fantasy, a soothing dream, completely opposed to our military experience, to the war, the anguish, and the extreme discomfort and privations of the desert. We strolled along Suleiman Pasha Avenue and looked at the storefronts in amazement and disbelief, and they did not arouse our envy, only our wonder and our imagination.

The prices were unattainable but despite this, we all bought three items: First, a robust shock-resistant watch to survive blows and sandstorms. Second, new shoes baptized "desert boots," although they had no relation to the desert. Made of sand-colored suede, with soft, comfortable soles, they contrasted sharply with our hard boots. They were the only shoes we were authorized to wear on our days off. The third item we bought was a desert scarf, made of wonderful soft Egyptian cotton, worn around the neck, and very useful to protect us from the desert sandstorms. With these three items – watch, shoes, and scarf – we felt invincible.

Dressed in our new acquisitions and a clean shirt with a starched collar, we dove into the ultimate adventure: to stroll in front of the elegant cafés and sit down at a table for a dry martini. The cafés had a front yard and a back garden with tables under the shade of large trees or umbrellas. They were the only places where Egyptians and British, civilians and military, mixed. They were also the only places where we could see beautiful, elegant, and desirable women.

The most famous café was Groppys. The women entered the café announcing their presence with their provocative and intoxicating perfume, the clicking of their high heels, their wide hats, the flirty scarves, the laces, and the brushing of their silk skirts against the edge of our table. They were experts. They never looked at us directly, but we fantasized that they watched us out of the corner of their eyes and noticed our manly presence. It was inconceivable for a British soldier to utter a compliment, even in low voice. It was considered bad manners and a disdainful "continental" custom. But we were too weak to control our feelings. We talked in French so as not to compromise the honor of the British Army. When an attractive girl passed by us, we would sigh conspicuously: "Oh la la! *Mon Dieu!*" How daring!

We anxiously scrutinized the face of the girl we liked. A glint in her eyes or a suppressed smile were for us the mark of a victory. The fine environment of the gardens, the umbrellas, the women, and the transparent air seemed to me like a dream, a living expression of the French Impressionist paintings I had seen in museums as a boy. It was an expensive experience, but it was worth the full price. When we returned to the war front, we recalled the garden scenes over and over, enjoying the reminiscence amid artillery duels, sandstorms, or suffocating heat.

We all suffered from nostalgia. Nostalgia for family, for familiar smells, for treasured food, for beloved landscapes of home. The elders among us were already three or four years away from their home and felt homesick in the African landscape and culture. I had only been in the army for one year, but when the Jewish high holidays approached, I also noticed the melancholy.

Al-Qahira Al-Yahud [Jewish Cairo]

Jewish Cairo was minuscule and became our refuge when we needed a familiar feel on a Jewish Shabbat. We rarely had an opportunity to talk to a civilian about topics unrelated to the war, but my friend Bobby, extroverted and witty, always discovered new opportunities. In Cairo he discovered Dr. Blum, an eminent physician from Berlin who had been called by King Farouk of Egypt to become his royal doctor. Only six Jewish families found asylum in Egypt in those years, and the Blum family was one of them. Bobby discovered that his grandfather had been Dr. Blum's patient in Berlin, and Dr. Blum, surprised, invited him for tea at his residence in the elegant Maadi district.

Bobby and I rang the bell at Dr. Blum's residence. A Sudanese servant emerged and guided us across the wide front yard to the main door. There, a second server took us through a large lobby to an elegant lounge with plush seating around copper embossed tables. Without a word, but with a wave of his hand, he invited us to take a seat and disappeared silently like a breath of wind. It was common among the wealthy in Cairo to have Sudanese as domestic staff. They were tall, slender men with gentle manners. Black as coal, their faces were inscrutable. They walked in giant, but measured steps, barefoot, and dressed in impeccable white robes. On the head, a plush turban with a bun of black silk, and around the waist, a colorful braided cloth.

The waiting room was sumptuous. Heavy tapestries hung from the walls, fluffy carpets covered the floor, and elaborate columns, sculptures and ivories adorned the room. As in all Arab houses, there were windows on opposite walls to create a breeze that cooled the hot air. Dr. Blum came in, plump and good-natured, and showed sincere joy in meeting us and in speaking in German. He asked for my last name, and we discovered he knew my father and his pharmacy. It was incredible to find an acquaintance here in Africa! Mr. Blum then clapped his hands, and a servant came in with a tray of Turkish coffee in long-stemmed glasses, and delicious German cakes prepared by Mrs. Blum herself. A delight to our palate! Dr. Blum was a rich man: as royal doctor he also attended to the Egyptian high society. He was known as "the German doctor," reflecting the Egyptians' sympathy for the Germans. We chatted for a long time and then departed with the promise of a new meeting. We were escorted back to the street by a small army of Sudanese servants.

The next reunion with Dr. Blum never took place. Five years later he left Egypt hastily to South Africa, at the start of Israel's war for independence. As six Arab states fought against Israel, there was no longer any room for a Jewish doctor in Egypt.

My friend Bobby also discovered a small synagogue in Cairo. We knew well the Jewish *mitzvah* [good deed] to welcome a traveler who shows up for the Shabbat service. Did not our patriarch Abraham welcome the three angels according to the Torah? One Friday night we attended the Shabbat service in the small synagogue and although we were not angels, we were warmly welcomed and invited to dine at one of the congregants' homes. Back in our barracks that night, we reviewed the experience: great food, warm hospitality, and cautious kindness. Our hosts were warm but feared that we might flirt with their daughters. Imagine a handsome military man with a heroic halo but poor, breaking the prevailing tradition of prudence. Our hosts were right: we were on a hunt and determined to apply our temporary attributes.

Bobby learned that the leader of this small congregation had two beautiful young daughters. We returned to the synagogue the next time we were in Cairo. We arrived armed with a new military stripe and our medals for defeating Rommel's Afrika Korps. Bobby asked for permission to take the daughters to the Victory Concert at the Cairo Theater, the most important social event of the moment. The gentleman noticed our boldness; he realized that a direct defense was not appropriate and opted for a strategic move. "Yes," he said, "I will allow them to join you, but you must also reserve a theater box for us, to preserve their good name." We could not but agree; we were trapped.

We bought the theater tickets. A major financial defeat, as the price consumed several months of our salary. On the day of the concert, the beautiful daughters sat with Bobby and me in the front row. Immediately behind us sat the parents to guarantee our exclusive dedication to the music and preclude the slightest sentimental detour. The concert was indeed spectacular: Beethoven's Fifth Symphony was the aural expression of victory, and Dvorak's New World Symphony fitted perfectly that moment in which we embraced dreams and hopes for a better world. Our love expectations, on the other hand, did not fare so spectacularly. At the end of the concert the family thanked us effusively and returned to their home. Bobby and I dropped on a bench in the theater garden, took a deep breath, and assessed our financial and sentimental defeat. As good soldiers, we decided to lower our aim and not to engage in additional religious activities. We swore to dedicate ourselves fully to mending our financial wounds.

Oh, Al-Qahira, so deeply etched in my memory!

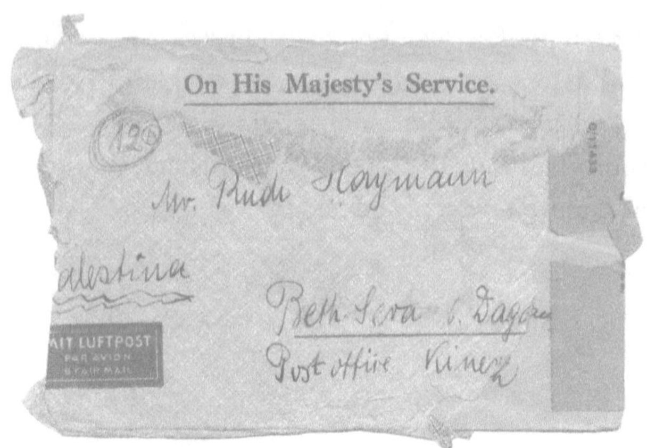

Envelope with the address amended and resent to reach me as I moved with my unit. First sent to MEF (Middle Eastern Forces) in Africa, then to CSDIC (Combined Services Detailed Interrogation Centre), and finally to CMF (Central Mediterranean Forces) in Italy.

WORDS THAT TRAVEL

1943–1944

Letters to soldiers, the thin thread of life,
moving across continents.

Mail was very slow and erratic during the war. My parents were thousands of miles away and thousands of war events derailed the mail. Of the many letters they wrote, only a few reached me, always with three or four months' delay. The letters were written in an old German *Sutterlin* calligraphy, on very thin, almost transparent paper, to reduce the postal cost, which was based on weight. Written in August 1941:

My dearest son: Another year in your life. You are turning 20 years today. We are far apart, and I cannot hold your head between my hands and kiss you endlessly for all the love you have missed. And when...? All I feel for you I want to express in this letter. You have lived without your parents' love during these years, and we are alone here in Chile. And around us, there are many broken families like us... But complaining does not help. We are immensely grateful that we are out of Germany and saved from all what is happening there. It is now more than six months without news from you, dear son...

This letter was sent to Beit-Zera, my kibbutz in British Palestine. However, six months earlier I had left the kibbutz to join the British Army and was now a soldier in the African war front. Due to the postal delays, my parents were still unaware of these key events. The next letter, dated October 1943, shows their reaction to the news. My father writes:

My dear son: So now you are a sergeant! Congratulations, we are very proud of you. My good boy, this is your duty, and you will know how to do your best. I always held on to the hope that your generation may grow up free of war but fate has willed it otherwise. From here afar, I can only concentrate all my good thoughts on you. I do wish we were living normal times...

We recently received news from your Onkel Fritz through the Red Cross. His letter took ten months to reach us. He is imprisoned in the Terezín Concentration Camp in Czechoslovakia. And your dear good Oma, whose most beloved child you were, passed away in December 1942 in Berlin. The news hurt us very much. This is the very first sign we have from our loved ones, in over a year; the first sign that Onkel Fritz is still alive. How he survives in those circumstances, we cannot even fathom... Unimaginable for us, who are so far away from where this terrible war is occurring.

And from my sister:

Dear brother: It is now five years since you left us, and four years since we arrived in Chile. And when will we be able to embrace you? I dream of walking proudly holding the arm of a handsome Sergeant of the British Jewish Brigade! Your July letter just arrived and gave us much joy. On November 1st I start a new job at a luggage manufacturing company, where I will earn a bit more money. I hope to like the new job, as I will forego my vacation for this change.

The next letter was dated 1944:

Dearest son: You can't imagine the great joy you gave us by sending us your photograph! I would have given everything for this picture. I look at your image and it reminds me of my father; you look like him. And your photograph also speaks to me about all what we have missed in these years. I grieve for not seeing you grow to become the fine man you now are. We missed out on our intimate conversations about life, which you liked so much. But I hold out hope that a time will come when we will be able to make up for this loss.

Chile is now officially at war as well. But, besides an increase in cost of living, this has no impact on daily life; it is peaceful here. A group of young volunteers departed recently to England to join the Allied Forces. As for me, I have lived enough wars in my life. The day will come, Rudi, when you will wear your civilian clothes again. But then, you will be a different person, because a war experience transforms a man. Take care of yourself, dear son. Much love from your Vati.

This last letter was directed to the "Middle East Forces" (MEF), the British Army unit in North Africa, where I started my service. But by the time the letter reached its destination, I had already left Africa, had landed in Italy, and was moving across Europe. The letter's envelope shows the successive address amendments made by the army censor, as the letter was resent to the Central Mediterranean Forces (CMF), following me throughout Europe, to finally reach me at my unit headquarters in Italy. The envelope also bears the initials "GSI" and "CSDIC," the special unit of the British Intelligence Service, in which I was serving, and for which no address could be disclosed.

The Landing in Anzio, Italy, January 22, 1944.

THE LANDING IN ANZIO-NETTUNO

ITALY, 1944

If they come to our shores,
they will perish in the surf.
Mussolini, 1943

We successfully completed the Africa campaign in mid-1943, and the Eighth British Army prepared for its next big task. On January 21,1944, we formed for roll call as usual at dawn. That day, the High Commander's Board listed my platoon number 775: we had been selected to participate in the expeditionary corps to land in Italy, with the mission of establishing a bridgehead behind the German lines. We had been training for this mission for three months.

The Allied armies in Italy were stalled at the Gustav Line, a mountainous and fortified line running across Italy at Monte Cassino, north of Naples. The combination of rugged terrain and enemy defenses made it impenetrable, and this had brought significant losses of men and material to our armies. Determined to restore our momentum, the Allied commanders planned Operation Shingle, a massive amphibious assault with 35,000 soldiers and 3,000 vehicles, that would land at the coastal towns of Anzio and Nettuno, 60 miles behind the enemy's Gustav Line. The goal was to strike inland to seize the high ground of the Alban Hills and cut the enemy supply lines. This assault, along with a simultaneous Allied attack on Monte Cassino, was expected to break the stalemate and enable the Allies to advance north to Rome.

We were scheduled to embark that same night. We, platoon commanders, were given aerial photographs of the beach towns of Anzio and Nettuno where we would disembark the next day. We were instructed on the route our units should take after disembarking, and on our military goal for the first day. We were also instructed on which ship we were to board: ours was LST 379.

Now I had to prepare my unit. In moments of combat, each soldier would take his military documents and minimal personal items in a small backpack, along with his load of weapons and ammunition. Like all Jewish soldiers of German origin, we wrote false information about our place of birth in our military passport. We did not know how the Nazis would act if we were taken prisoners. I also distributed special envelopes to the men to send a letter to their family before leaving for combat.

We then set off along the two-kilometer road to the coast. Going downhill, we spotted the two dozen huge boats waiting for us on the beach. Ours, LST 379, was one of the largest, three decks high and loaded with heavy machinery, tanks, and supply trucks. The officer in charge directed us to the third deck. The ship had no windows.

As soon as we embarked, all doors closed. The engines began to roar, and the ship backed off the beach. From the noise of the engines, we could tell we were at sea. Sea-mine sweepers preceded our expeditionary flotilla to clear our path, and we navigated surrounded by warships to protect us from enemy E-boats and submarines. We were informed that a hot meal would be served, and that hot tea would be available all night. No alcohol was allowed.

I identified a good space for my troop and prepared myself for what was to come. Everyone was nervous, but I was the most nervous. I was only 22, and this was my first time commanding a platoon of 32 soldiers in a major operation. It was a huge responsibility to take 32 young men into battle, and even more so in an amphibious landing.

I thought of Maxi, a fantastic man who had been our platoon commander before me during our first landing south of Naples. He had been promoted and I was appointed to replace him. So here I was, trying to fit into my new role. Maxi had taught me that in moments of calm, the commander can enjoy some advantages, but in times of combat, action, or emergency, it is the commander who steps in first and attends to everyone else, playing the role of leader, father, and server all at the same time.

Half of my unit was composed of veterans who had known each other for over half a year. The other half were novices who had come to replace those who had been lost in battle. I encouraged my men to stay calm, to sleep and rest, to be in their best condition for the early morning landing, which would demand our total attention and maximum effort.

The soldiers formed small groups. One group sat in a circle, sharing family photographs and keeping their loved ones in mind: "These are my parents," "This is my girlfriend," "These are my children." One man led a group of men who pretended to feel no emotion; they played cards, betting six months of their pay. But they knew it was pretense, because if you do not survive, you do not pay; and if you survive but your partner does not, who will pay you? And if you both survive, would you demand payment after the experience of battle?

In the third group were the withdrawn. Some wrote a letter to their loved ones, pondering if this might be their last one. Others filled the last page of their military passport, the one entitled "My last will." Meanwhile, my vice-commander Michael and I attended to all. We distributed cups of tea to help keep bodies and spirits warm; we said some kind words; we took care of our men to allow them to focus on their personal issues. And thus, the hours passed. The sea was calm, the lights were dim, and the men began to fall asleep.

I have asked myself many times if I was afraid. On my first sea crossing months before, I had felt fear; the fear of drowning in the sea if we were hit by a German torpedo. Just recently a ship like ours had been torpedoed despite the protection of the warships surrounding it, and we lost 140 of our comrades. But this time I was not afraid. Maybe because the possibility of being discovered by the Germans was low on that day; maybe the surprise factor of our operation gave me a sense of security; or maybe I was rising to the leader role. I do not know. The fact is that I was not afraid.

Finally, the moment arrived. The lights turned on, and through the loudspeakers we were instructed to get ready and use the bathroom for the last time. Our commander spoke: "In 20 minutes we will arrive at the beachhead and disembark. The sea is calm; the sun will rise in ten minutes; we have overcast skies." Overcast skies. Magical words.

Overcast skies meant that we would be spared the worst threat to a landing: the German Stuka planes. No other aircraft terrorized a landing expedition as much as these dive bombers with their machine guns sowing death from above. If the clouds hung low, the Stukas could not see their targets, nor could they descend below the clouds to sow death among us. There could not be better news.

One might expect that upon hearing this, everyone would jump up and cheer. But no, this was the British Army, and the British did not display their emotions. Although everyone felt great relief, not a sound was uttered. My soldiers closed their lips tightly into a thin line and swallowed their emotion. Many looked down so as not give away with their eyes, what they hid with their mouths.

In a few minutes the landing would begin. Our commander wished us good luck. "See you at the day's end, in kilometer eight."

We faced the front of the ship where three lights displayed the instructions. First a red light turned on, signaling us to approach the vehicle that each one had been assigned for disembarkation. We all got up, grabbed our bags and our guns, descended the metal ladder to the lower deck and sat on a tank, a cannon, a cargo vehicle, or – in the case of my unit – on our motorcycles.

Five minutes later a yellow light turned on, signaling us to start our vehicles' engines. What a tremendous roar, what a deafening noise! Dozens and dozens of tanks, trucks, motorcycles, and other vehicles roaring within the ship's enclosed deck. It seemed as if the ship would explode. The yellow light also signaled us to hold on firmly, as the ship engines roared up and the ship rammed the beach with maximum force. A huge jolt, a sudden jam, a hard blow that threw us from our positions.

The first ray of light appeared as the front doors of the ship opened and the bridge was lowered. Then, a green light turned on at the center, indicating that the central row should disembark. Soon the green light turned on in front of our own line. I raised my arm, and my men and I accelerated on our motorbikes, riding out arrow-fast onto the beach.

And there we went, over the pontoon in two straight rows, one led by Michael, one led by me, crossing the beach at the highest speed we could. In front of us, the destroyed village of Anzio. We took a 45-degree angle to the right and rode uphill at full speed, fast, very fast. Ahead, a gentle hill. We rode up and up. Everything seemed calm.

On top of the hill, I ordered our first stop. We turned off the engines, reclined the motorcycles, and urinated. The intense tension of the last hours had created enormous pressure and we all needed to relieve ourselves. I looked back at the beach, far behind us. It was full of soldiers and war machinery. Everything had been disembarked, and the huge vessels were retreating to sea to go back for a second contingent.

Up here, all was quiet, and it seemed that we would advance at a good speed. We mounted our motorbikes again, more confident, more willing to do anything and everything.

But nobody, absolutely nobody, suspected the hell that was waiting for us ahead.

In the trenches.

Medics attending to an injured soldier, 1944.

THE BATTLE FOR ROME
ITALY, 1944

German airborne war pamphlet dropped over British troops

"Happy landing. See you at kilometer eight," our commander had said as we landed on the beach. His words still resonated in my ears. The happy landing seemed to be true. No terrifying German Stuka planes were waiting for us; no intense fire or mortar was coming from the surrounding hills.

We kept going on our motorbikes. Everything was calm and quiet – maybe too quiet. We rode to the northeast following our commander's instructions, advancing at good speed. At this rate, we would arrive sooner than expected to our first goal. And then, a gentle rain began to fall. Within an hour the land around had saturated; the waters did not drain, the soil softened, and we got stuck in the mud with our motorbikes. Bewildering. We had landed in a huge swamp. No wonder we had not encountered military resistance; the Germans never imagined that our strategists would commit the folly of planting us in this place.

But we had to continue moving, no matter what obstacles we found. With much work and much suffering, we reached the village of Aprilia the next day, where we encountered intense German resistance. "Entrenching!" was the order. We had too many rifles and no shovels. We requisitioned all available shovels from the Italian peasants and dug trenches in the soft ground, but they filled with water in minutes. It rained and rained incessantly for days and days, and then for weeks and weeks. We were wet, trapped, and under constant fire.

Reinforcements arrived with a second landing. More tanks, more ammunition, more heavy material. But everything sank in this enormous swamp. Stuck in the quag, we were unable to expand our action, unable to free land for the supplies and the troops that came behind us, and unable to complete our mission. Our goal was to open a bridgehead to penetrate inland bypassing the German-held Gustav Line, and advance north to capture Rome. We were supposed to arrive within two weeks at the gates of the great city. But instead, it took us 17 weeks.

The Germans, commanded by Field Marshal Kesselring, took advantage of our situation, fortifying their lines, strengthening their defenses, and bombarding us non-stop. Fierce battles ensued. The Germans had a clear view of our positions and knew that each bomb would hit us, given our inability to move, disperse, or advance. They tried to push us back to the sea, but we resisted well. They turned our life into hell, bombing us incessantly, subjecting us to constant artillery, mortar, or small arms fire. For three months we resisted, buried in the mud, entrenched, wet, and numb. We had no choice but to wait for the end of the winter rains and for the land to dry, to be able to advance and fulfill our mission.

In this long resistance battle I was wounded for the first time. A German shell hit our canned food storage, shredding the cans into a thousand splinters that showered on us. Three splinters hit my right leg. The field doctor's extraction of the shrapnel hurt more than the injury.

Colonel Roberts, our commander, commissioned me to coordinate with our four gunner units. I reached the first unit, jumped into their trench, and instructed the sergeant in charge. It was pouring when I reached the second unit. "Comrade, come into our tent and share our tea until the downpour stops," offered the sergeant. I happily accepted. Drinking hot tea was the soldier's way to keep both, body and spirit warm. And while we drank, we talked.

There were two recurrent topics of conversation: survival stories and concern for our families. We trusted that we could take care of ourselves at the front, but we worried much about our families. Our worries were fueled by the lack of news or mail. When mail finally arrived, the recipient would check the address anxiously: Had it changed? Had the family been bombed or evacuated? Each soldier would express his sorrows to the receptive ear of his companions, seeking support to endure this very long war. "What about your family?" I was asked. "Man," I said, "my parents managed to escape to South America; a miracle." "Where to?" asked the corporal in charge of the sextant. "To the farthest corner, a long, thin country called Chile.'" "Chile? I am Chilean, grandson of English immigrants and I volunteered for this war." A small world, indeed.

One hundred days after our landing, the endless rains finally ceased. We got out of our wet trenches and resumed our mission. Aprilia, the village where we had been entrenched, was now a pile of rubble, its population escaped to Campania and Calabria. The Allied armies that had been stuck at the Gustav Line, also began their assault on the Line in May 1944, to link up with our breakout forces. The simultaneous breakthrough and breakout of our Allied armies allowed us to finally move north.

The battles we endured in Anzio and on the Gustav Line resulted in 98,000 Allied casualties and 60,000 Axis casualties. Such is the human cost of war.

As we advanced, I shifted my focus to intelligence work. There are three critical items that a war commander needs when taking his troops to combat: first, the strength, willpower, and combative drive of his people; second, timely supplies; and third, solid intelligence information. And this last critical aspect was my responsibility in this Italian campaign.

We wanted to win the battles with the fewest casualties, whether injured, captured, or dead. We all wanted to return home alive. The more information we had about our enemy, the better our leaders could strategize and reduce our losses. Knowing the number, strength, equipment, supply lines, and plans of our enemy was crucial to winning a battle. Getting that information on the front line was my job: obtaining it in abundance, with precision, speed, and on the spot, for our commanders to make successful combat decisions.

We were a group of four intelligence officials, with prior experience from the Africa campaign. Michael was the son of a British military attaché in Berlin and Moscow and spoke perfect German and Russian. Hamish was Scottish, with studies in European history, and spoke Italian and German. Dov and I were born and raised in Germany, lived in a kibbutz, trained in the Haganah, and spoke German and Italian. We had been recruited to be part of the British Counter-Intelligence Corps (CIC) because of our knowledge of our enemies' languages.

Our work was highly sensitive and required sound judgment. The Geneva Convention instructed prisoners to provide their personal and unit identification and prohibited the captor from obtaining information through force or torture. The British Army was extremely respectful of international conventions; the German prisoners knew this well, and tried to provide minimal information.

We debated how to proceed. Request formal authorization? It would be denied. Accept minimal information? A failure to our commanders, who urgently needed information. We would never torture a helpless prisoner, no matter how much we hated him; but we also knew that the information we gathered saved the lives of our own soldiers. In the front line there is no time for sophisticated cross-examinations; there is urgency; it is yes or no, now or never. We opted for reasonable "pressure." It provided results and did not go against our conscience. We examined our conscience again and again, contrasting it with the needs of our troops, our values, and our role in this war. We had volunteered to defeat Nazism; we were on the front line with the combat troops because of the peculiar condition of our German origin and our command of languages. This was our work; it had to be done well, and we did it.

We ordered the German soldiers to empty their pockets. Their contents often provided good information – written orders, dates, places. But we needed more, much more. We resorted to the letters from their children, the photos of their wives or brides, their war amulets for good fortune. Nothing is more treasured by a soldier, on both sides of the line of fire, than these personal items. The letters from your parents are your bulletproof breastplate, the photos of your children are your iron armor; they are the magic that protects you and gives you the strength to resist.

We took these elements of great sentimental value from the prisoners. "I asked you a question, you don't want to answer? What if I tear this letter? What if I pee on your girlfriend's photo? What if I throw it in the latrine?" Does this sound cruel? Yes, in today's ethos. But those were war times. It worked, and we did it. We did it because we did not want to write letters that said: "Dear Mrs. Johnson, as platoon commander, I am sorry to inform you that your son has not returned..." In times of peace, decades later, it sounds terrible. But in those war years, human values were tested to the extreme, turned over; every action was a matter of life or death. Psychological pressure was nothing compared with a soldier mutilated or killed by an enemy minefield that we failed to discover.

Each captured soldier had the right to send a preprinted Red Cross card to his family, notifying them that he had been taken prisoner. This card had enormous value. You had been taken prisoner and torn away from your unit. After the initial shock and fear, you realized it was not so terrible. For you, the war was over; you were now a prisoner of the British. They would not hurt you; they would feed you, and in one or two years you would go back home. Alive. Unhurt. Being a prisoner of the British was appreciated, as it assured survival. You wanted your family to know this as soon as possible, because before the Red Cross card reached your family, they would receive a card from the German Army: "Private X did not return to his unit today May 1, 1944. Condition: dead or unknown. Signed, the Commander." Receiving this card was the worst blow to a family, submerging them in the fear that you were dead.

Thus, every prisoner wanted their Red Cross card to be sent as soon as possible, to turn their family's anguish into relief. "Did you ask for the Red Cross card? Wait, maybe next week. Where was the location of the minefield? Strengthen your memory before I send your signed card." We saved many lives, and we contributed to the Nazi defeat.

It was May 1944, and the end of the war was not yet in sight. News was leaking to our troops about the Nazi concentration camps. Terrifying news – about death camps, about mass extermination of Jews. Our hatred grew. Yes, hatred from us, Jewish soldiers. The British soldiers saw in the German troops a fierce adversary, but we, Jewish soldiers, felt hatred growing. I followed the British rules, but I was conflicted internally.

There was more. The mail to and from my parents was scant and erratic. My mother wrote: "Rudi, we have not heard from you for over six months. We can only hope you are alive." "Beloved son, for four years we have not heard from our family trapped in Germany. Does this mean the worst…?" My parents were suffering without news from their son in the war. And here, on the battlefield, a German prisoner demanded that I send news to his family in six hours? The prisoners appealed to our "humanitarian sense." But what about my mother's suffering waiting for her son's news? What about my father without news from his brother trapped in Germany? My blood was boiling. Remorse? None. Only unpleasant memories.

In May 1944, we finally started our great offensive towards Rome. By then, we had taken hundreds, thousands of prisoners. We totally changed our tactics and goals. There was no time for complicated questions. We now asked only two questions: "How far have you been ordered to fall back?" and "Have you been ordered to defend Rome?" We wanted to know what lay ahead for the conquest of Rome. Our information indicated that the Germans would retreat, and the city would be saved from destruction.

We could not handle the large number of prisoners anymore, so we asked for reinforcements. They sent us Teo. Teo was older, a cold and calculating man whose outlook had been shaped by rough life experiences. Teo came up with a new strategy. All our recent prisoners carried some Italian money, for which they would have no use in the prisoner camps. Teo set four cardboard boxes on the floor, each with a sign: 10, 50, 100, 500 liras. He then lined up the prisoners and asked them to empty their pockets in the boxes before proceeding to hand them their Red Cross cards. The cardboard boxes filled up. There was no time to count. Instead, Teo divided the booty of each box into six stacks weighted down with a stone and redistributed the bills until all stacks were the same height. Done.

We had been crouching in the swamp for 17 weeks; with this booty we would live like princes in Rome for 17 weeks.

The end of the heavy fighting and the suffering was close. It was June 1944; Rome's silhouette was now on the horizon.

British troops entering Rome, June 5, 1944.

LIBERATION

ROME, 1944

When thou drawest nigh unto a city to fight against it,
first proclaim peace unto it.
Deuteronomy 20:10

The day was dawning, but I had been awake for hours, wrapped in my blankets in my tent, surrounded by dozens of sleeping soldiers. I was enjoying a precious moment, a forgotten feeling: complete silence.

For 17 weeks since we had disembarked at Anzio, we had not had one night without the deep rumble of heavy artillery and the high-pitched sound of light weapons. For months we had suffered torrential rains and the fierce resistance of our enemy. We were utterly exhausted. But we had just glimpsed for the first time the silhouette of Rome.

As the first rays of light crept over the horizon, we formed our battalion. This was a very special day: tomorrow we would finally enter the city of Rome victoriously.

The liberation of Rome was of strategic military importance because of its airfields and extensive road and rail networks. It was the first European capital to be freed from Nazi rule and was therefore hugely significant in regaining the Allies' stronghold in

Europe. Our entry to Rome would be the crowning achievement of my unit, the First British Infantry Division, and for the 56th London Division, after our enormous effort during the last four months of combat.

Rome had been under German occupation since September 1943. Pope Pius XII had articulated an agreement between Germans and Allies to protect Rome from destruction, calling it *città aperta* [open city], meaning the Allies would not bomb it and the Germans would not defend it, retreating north instead. Both sides had abided by the agreement.

I was summoned to a meeting at the Intelligence Service Advanced Headquarters in the town of Castel Gandolfo on the outskirts of Rome. The magnificent building had been saved from damage, as it was in the shadow of the Pope's summer residence, and the Vatican territory and its immediate surroundings were considered inviolable. Up until three days prior, this magnificent palace had been used as a German Officers' Club.

I parked my faithful Matchless motorcycle in the elegant cobblestoned front yard. What a pleasure it was to see comrades alive whom I had not seen in eight months! But the best was to see Eric, my friend, part of a ring of five who had forged a deep friendship, as only war can do. We had joined the Intelligence Service together, but we were completely different. Eric was six years older than me and had studied hospitality in a Swiss school before the war. I, on the other hand, had not even completed high school and was a kibbutz pioneer.

The palace's large carved doors opened, and Captain Middleton invited us into the spacious hall. Sir Harold Macmillan, the British Minister Resident in the Mediterranean, who would later succeed Churchill as British prime minister, walked in. "Gentlemen," he began. We knew that in addressing us, low-ranking officers, as "gentlemen," he was asking for exceptional execution of the task ahead.

"Tomorrow we will enter Rome triumphantly," he said. "It will be a historic day – the first European capital to be liberated – and the world's eyes will be on us. Our combined British and American troops add up to over 35,000 soldiers and organizing this mass of men for a seamless occupation is a major challenge. We must do this with outmost care and without dismantling civilian life. We will form several commissions to administer the city during the first days, until specialized personnel arrive. The civilian aspects will be handled by the American Army, and we, the British Army, will be responsible for all technical and semi-military elements. You, Intelligence Officers, will lead these commissions, each with 30 military officers. At the end of the day tomorrow, each of you will submit your report at the Hotel Flora on the Via Venetto. I promise you a bed and a hot shower."

We were all silent, impressed, and proud of the role we would play in this historic event.

But the best news for us, exhausted soldiers, was the magic words "hot shower." Hot shower! A pleasure we had completely forgotten in the last four months. We sat there, with half-closed eyes, gently rocking and dreaming of the wonderful sensation of a jet of hot water on our bodies, slowly dissolving the layers on our skin: the outer layer of mud and dirt accumulated in four months, then the layer of sweat adhering to our pores, until finally reaching our true skin. A sublime sensation, like an act of love that we enjoy first imagining, then executing, and finally recalling.

The dry voice of Captain Middleton pulled us back from our musings, as he announced the commissions. "First Commission: Potable Water," responsible for securing water for the population. "Second Commission: Light and Power," responsible for electric supply and sabotage prevention. "Third Commission: Fascist Party Headquarters," tasked with occupying the building and recovering documentation. "Fourth Commission: Prison," responsible for preventing riots and separating criminals from political prisoners.

Finally, it was Eric's and my turn: "Fifth Commission: Sanitary." My heart dropped; I hated hospitals... what bad luck. Captain Middleton handed us the address of the Hotel Flora, the police detachment code, two maps of Rome, and a list with 14 addresses. "These are Rome's brothels. Your task is to close them all down and keep them under control until the medics arrive for check-ups, to prevent disease among the troops." My heart was beating again.

Eric and I settled in an elegant side room to prepare our plan. We extended our map on one of the tables and marked the Hotel Flora, and the north–south axis of the Via Appia, which the British Army would follow when entering Rome. We decided that Eric would take on the brothels west of the Via Appia and I would take those on the east side. The two brothels located in the center would be covered by the one who arrived first. We would then meet at the last point, near Piazza di Spagna, to write our report and take it to the Hotel Flora.

With our fingers, we followed the sinuous line of the Tevere River on the map, looking for yet another place: the Great Synagogue of Rome at the Piazza di Tempio. We circled it carefully in pen. Yes, this would also be a target for us tomorrow. Because each soldier wages two wars: the official war, and his personal war, which can take many forms: collect as many medals as possible or conquer the most female hearts. Our private war was the Jewish war. Terrible news was filtering through the front lines: rumors of mass deportations of Jews, forced labor, and annihilation in death camps. We heard about tens of thousands, and even hundreds of thousands. We did not fathom that it would be millions. The news gave us goosebumps and made our blood run cold.

We had joined the British Army to defeat Nazi Germany and save people. The official war seemed too slow, and I felt I had not done very well in my personal war. After five months of fighting in North Africa my platoon reached Tripoli ten hours after its ghetto of detained Jews was liberated. I regretted not having been the first to arrive. Months later, north of Naples, we arrived at Torre Annunciata. The town was totally devastated, and its population had been evacuated. And then, from the ruins emerged a group of emaciated figures, human ghosts, raising their hands in surrender. Fourteen Jews had hidden in the barrels of a wine factory that had miraculously withstood the bombs. We gave them water, food, blankets, and human warmth, and then entrusted them to the Red

Cross team that arrived after us. The war continued; we had to go on.

I dreamt of liberating many, hundreds. Now I would be one of the first Jews to arrive in Rome and liberate the Nazi-ruled city. By marking the Piazza di Tempio on our map, we drew a small frame for our grand dream.

The great day began at four-thirty in the morning, June 5, 1944. I was so excited that I could not close my eyes all night. For the umpteenth time I checked the wire stand that I had improvised on my motorcycle to hold the map of Rome. I started my motorcycle again to ensure this very faithful friend was running smoothly and would not fail me at this historic moment. At five-thirty in the morning the troops were ready, and this huge military force began to move. We entered Rome as the day dawned and by six o'clock, we were flooding the centuries-old Via Appia. And there, among the thousands and thousands of soldiers, was my little column: a truck with 30 military men, a jeep, and I, in front of them, on my motorcycle with the map of Rome tied to my steering bar.

The Via Appia was a mythical name for me. I had learned in school about this marvel of Roman engineering built in 312 b.c. Spanning 563 kilometers, it was the Roman super-highway, used by the armies traveling to conquer territories for the empire. Roman troops returned to Rome on this road, loaded with glory and treasures plundered in faraway latitudes. The victorious generals erected triumphal arches to celebrate their conquests. The Arch of Titus stands precisely where the Via Appia enters the Roman Forum, and in its bas-reliefs are the Roman legionaries holding up the menorah, the candelabra symbol of the Jewish temple in Jerusalem that the Romans destroyed in the year A.D. 70 during the Bar Kokhba revolt. And behind the legionaries walk the chained prisoners, the defeated, to be sold as slaves in Rome. "*Hierosolyma est perdita*" [Jerusalem is destroyed] sang the soldiery. And to remove all traces of Jewish resistance and identity in their land, Emperor Hadrian changed the name of the Land of Judea to Land of Philistines.

All this history rushed back to my memory as I entered Rome

with my unit. Titus entered Rome in the year 70, and I would pass victoriously under this same arch today. Would my youthful dream become real and this day be recorded in the history books? Rudi, keep your thoughts under your steel helmet, you have war tasks to do.

As we reached the Via dei Fiori, I raised my right arm to signal to my small column to veer right, away from the Via Appia and the huge human mass. As we moved away, the heavy metallic noise of the troops became an undefined murmur, like the sound of the sea from afar.

The Via Piccione was quiet and empty. There was not a soul, not a dog or cat in sight on the street. The Romans were hiding behind closed shutters. Certainly, no one was sleeping; everyone was peering out from behind their shutters, as no one knew yet if there would be fighting in the streets. We stopped our vehicles in front of number 57. I knocked on the door. No response. I knocked harder. Still no response. I shouted in Italian, threatening to tear down the door. A female voice responded: "What do you want, sir? This is a peaceful house." "All is fine, miss, I beg you to open." "No," said the voice. "This is a peaceful private house." "Miss," I said, "this is the British Military Police." As soon as I uttered these words, she responded, "Death to fascism, long live democracy!" "I do not need a political manifesto, miss, I need you to let me in. You are not in danger."

Finally, the door opened. A woman in a white gown was on the threshold. Her face turned paler than her gown when she saw us with our steel helmets and armed to the teeth. She let me into the waiting room, which was furnished with a row of chairs set against the wall, facing a long carpet that served as a catwalk. The woman trembled, murmuring Hail Marys, fearing this was her final hour. I had intended to explain to her the new regulations, but seeing her fear, I first calmed her down and asked her to gather the house residents. She clapped her hands, the corridor doors opened, and a dozen young women filed out dressed in their "work clothes", displaying their voluptuous busts and butts. The situation had changed radically: my knees were now weak and trembling. I tried to regain my composure as a messenger of "His Royal Majesty" and explained the new rules, instructing the women on the strict prohibition on dispensing their favors to our troops until the medical review. Then I proceeded to close the premises, leaving three soldiers on duty. Never in the war did so many men volunteer for duty. It also took some effort to get the rest of my soldiers back onto our truck.

The situation was similar in the next two houses. By the time we reached the fourth, it had become clear to all Romans that there would be no fighting in the streets and that this would be a glorious and splendid day. Rome's entire population of a million and a half took to the streets to see, celebrate, and cheer the Allied troops. The joy of liberation!

At midday I completed the tour of brothels on my list and advanced to Rome's center. I was mesmerized by the beauty of this city. I crossed the Piazza Colonna and went on to the Piazza di Spagna, Rome's most beautiful, with its famous steps and the Trinitá dei Monti, to reach the very last brothel on our list. My pal Eric had gotten there ahead of me; a guard was already at the door of the elegant five-story building. I entered the lobby and looked around, surprised; this place was clearly of a different class, elegant and luxurious. I was a naïve kibbutz pioneer and had never seen anything like this. The space was richly decorated in red velvet, with gilded frames, heavy curtains, ornaments, and plump armchairs. Through the windows I saw the great bustle and thunder of the troops and the masses on the streets, while here inside a deep tranquility reigned.

A minute later, Eric showed up in a silk robe, shaved, showered, and perfumed. I was speechless. "You're late, old man," he said. "Welcome to your new home. We will be well attended to here." Seeing my shocked face and hearing me argue that we should work on our report, he said, "Rudi, when will you stop being a *Schwitzer*, a *Haluzt*, a hard-working pioneer? Come, enjoy life, relax. Why would you be with hundreds of stinking soldiers if there are lovely, perfumed girls here? Do as I do, take a bath and let one of these beauties brush your back."

We were so different! I reflected and said, "Eric, you may be right, but we have yet another mission." "I know," he replied. "Let's relax and then we'll go." "No," I said, "I will do it the other way around. I will do my mission first, and then relax here as you advise."

I jumped onto my motorcycle, crossed the city center and the impossibly crowded Piazza Venezia, and headed towards the banks of the Tevere River, passing the Circus Maximus. And there it was, imposing and splendid, facing a square on the Via di Tempio, the Great Synagogue of Rome. Not a soul was there.

Half a block away, the Via Lungotevere was drowned in the agitated movement of the troops and the cheering crowds. But here in this hidden square, nobody. I crossed the space to get closer to the enormous building with its shining squared dome. I had never seen such a building; an eclectic and wild mix of Roman cathedral and Assyrian palace with Art Nouveau details. The main facade featured four tall columns and huge carved wooden doors. Everything was closed. I walked around to observe the building's riverside façade. A sign was posted on the door, featuring a skull and two crossed bones with text in German and Italian: "*Lebensgefahr/Pericolo de vita*" [Mortal danger]. This building is mined. Strictly forbidden to enter." Signed below: "Sturmbannführer Herbert Kappler," Rome's Nazi Police Commander.

Here I was, touching the temple wall. A feeling of sad solitude hung in the air. I was a bit disillusioned; I thought I would find people here, but it was barely a few hours since we had entered Rome, and Jews would still be in hiding. I looked at the columns of troops marching along the Via Lungotevere and noticed two figures stepping from the troop lines and approaching the temple. They were British soldiers; they looked at the building and consulted their map like I had done earlier. They greeted me from afar and, as good Britons, did not approach me. A moment later a jeep arrived with two Americans, who got out, walked around the building, then looked at me and came to shake my hand. "Hello" they said. "Where are you coming from?" I showed them my Palestine

Regiment badge. "Oh, really?" We exchanged some words and they left. I stayed another while in silence.

I went back to join Eric in the luxurious brothel to write our report. We dropped it at the Hotel Flora in the late afternoon as instructed. "Unfortunately, there are no more beds available here," we were told. "No problem" we replied, "we have a good place to stay."

The next day I was appointed public relations assistant, in charge of organizing the Victory Concerts by the Band of Pipers of the 51st Highland Division. The series of concerts would take place throughout Rome's most iconic spaces: the Roman Forum, the Piazza Venezia, the Piazza San Pietro, and the Colosseum. How excited I was to visit all these amazing historic spaces!

In between my work tasks I went back to the Great Synagogue. The situation had changed completely: civilians, survivors, and soldiers had gathered there and were shaking hands, embracing, and celebrating. The synagogue, however, could not be accessed until the mines were dismantled. I joined the celebration and was profusely embraced as the only member of the Jewish Brigade. It felt truly special to be there in that magical moment.

In a building adjacent to the synagogue there was a small space, which the Germans did not discover, and the Italians did not denounce, where the *Sifrei* Torah, the Jewish ceremonial scrolls, had been hidden. Thirty Jews had hidden there and had been saved from the deportations that had taken place in Rome in 1943. On that day, we prayed two *tefilot* [prayers] in the little space: *Shehecheyanu*, the gratitude prayer to thank for the privilege of reaching this day; and a *Kaddish* [mourning prayer], for all the Jews deported to concentration camps and for the fallen soldiers of this war.

Claudia, my first love, Rome, 1944.

LOVE IN ROME
ROME, 1944

Kiss me. Kiss me as if it were the last time.
Ingrid Bergman in *Casablanca*, 1942

In June 1944 I experienced a new milestone in my life: my first vacation in over five years – ten full days to linger, sleep late, and enjoy.

After two nights in Rome's most luxurious brothel, I had found that it lost much of its initial appeal, and I searched for a new home. I discovered the Pensione Elguetta in the Piazza del Gesù, just a few steps from the Piazza Venezia. The Pensione had been requisitioned to house the Scottish Regiment Band of Pipers, whose Victory Concerts I was in charge of organizing. The band's director, my friend Captain Henderson, had suggested it. It was a quiet place, removed from the urban bustle. But twice a day the Pensione's tranquility was broken. In my public relations role at the band's concerts, I explained to the public the details of Scottish music, uniforms, and customs, including the fact that the Scots do not wear undergarments under their kilts. The band director then inspected the skirted men with a small mirror attached to the tip of a cane to ensure they comply with this tradition. This aroused the curiosity of Rome's people, who gathered in the Piazza del Gesù to watch up close this unique ritual twice a day.

I went to pick up my mail. There were two letters from my family in Chile. I checked the stamps: they had been posted four months ago. They wrote about their efforts and tribulations to rebuild their lives in Chile and their worries about me; they knew I was at the front, but they had had no news from me. "Rudi, dear, we pray you are healthy; it is now six months since we last heard from you." How many sleepless nights had my mother suffered? What could I do? Nothing, while I was at the war front. But now I was in Rome. I decided to go to the Chilean Embassy at the Vatican. "May I talk to the ambassador?" I asked. "Yes sir, you can." I introduced myself with my military passport: P/38691 Sergeant Haymann, commander of Platoon 775 of the Third Battalion. The ambassador, in turn, gave me his card: Mr. Luiz Cruz Ocampo, ambassador of the Republic of Chile to the Holy See. "Mr. Ambassador, at the outbreak of the war my parents were lucky to leave Europe and be welcomed into Chile. They're fine, but extremely worried about me, as they haven't heard from me for six months. Is there some way you could you help?"

Mr. Ocampo opened his desk drawer, pulled out pen and paper, pushed them towards me, and said, "Write two sentences, Sergeant; I will send the message as a Vatican diplomatic telegram." I wrote: "Dear parents: don't worry about me. I'm safe and healthy. Rudi." And the miracle: a few days later the telegram reached my parents in Chile. Mr. Ocampo produced in 24 hours what the mail could not do in 24 weeks. My parents promptly replied:

Stato de la Citta del Vaticano – Telegramma. Parents and sister of Rudolf Haymann happy about telegram. All healthy. Letters written via Algiers with picture arrived. Ludwig Haymann.

The Pensione's owner and her daughters catered to me like a king. They served me breakfast, made my bed, and washed my clothes. My vacation felt dreamlike. I slept in late and then joined the "Boy meets girl" scene in the wonderful Il Pincio park that linked the elegant Via Vittorio Veneto with the Piazza del Popolo. Under the park's grove of trees, Italian girls and American, English, and French soldiers strolled from one end to the other, in search of each other. We were all young. We had all been through a ravaging war. Now we had shaved, we wore clean, starched shirts, shiny boots, and our army badges. We were ready to conquer.

My friend Teo, older and daring, organized our outings. I was shy, but here at Il Pincio park, luck was guaranteed. It was entertaining and easy, since we spoke perfect Italian. Teo looked for sexiness; I looked for exquisiteness. I learned a lot. Sometimes we won only sweet fugitive kisses; other times, with patience and well-planned work, much more. All the young women were beautiful and friendly. As I now review my war diary, I am surprised by the number of girls I met, whose names I wrote down, but whom I never called back. Alba, a post office employee, vital and ready to engage in romance, but boring after our third encounter. Paola was a beauty of calm and measured manners, but I had no patience for her slow talk. Elena was a cultured and gifted artist, who had her studio in the Via Margutta, near the Piazza di Spagna; she introduced me to many well-known and emerging artists, which I will always be very grateful for. But she was so stiff that I wasn't sure if I was with the artist or the canvas figure.

One day, Teo and I met two beautiful girls in the park. One was blond, daring, and outgoing. "Mine," claimed Teo. The other was a beautiful brunette with blue eyes that looked down shyly. "I'll take her," I said. Prophetic. Claudia and I stayed together until I left Italy, 20 months later. She was 17 and was studying art. We were perfectly congenial and never tired of each other.

My precious ten-day vacation ended, and I returned to the service. The British Intelligence Service had moved its headquarters to Rome, specifically, to Cinecittà on Via Aurelia. Cinecittà was a large film studio complex created by Mussolini in 1937 to house the School of Cinema and Propaganda to promote his fascist ideals. Designed in a sleek early Modernist style, the elegant building featured double-height columns on the facade and a magnificent hall clad in black and white marble, with a frieze inscribed with the phrase: "*Il cinema e l'arma piu forte, Mussolini* [Cinema is the most powerful weapon, Mussolini.]"

The British colonels and generals wanted to be in the very best place and had chosen wisely. The building's 22 luxury dressing rooms became the offices for our senior officers. The rest of the dressing rooms, less luxurious but still comfortable, each with its own lavatory, shower, and toilet, were designated for us, two per room. Never since I had left Germany five years ago had I enjoyed such luxury and privacy; not in the kibbutz, not in the Haganah, and not in the army.

Other sections of the vast Cinecittà campus were used to house displaced persons: one camp for refugees from Italy, Libya and Dalmatia and another for international refugees from Yugoslavia, Poland, Egypt, Iran, and China.

My friend Eric introduced me to his most recent and notorious prisoner: Herbert Kappler, SS colonel and former Chief of Nazi Security Police and Security Service in Rome. He had been the brain and organizer of arrests and deportations to concentration camps, mass executions, and innumerable atrocities. A human beast. He did not show remorse, did not apologize or ask for leniency. He was proud and mocked us, calling us chickens, because we did not kill him but instead, gave him shelter and food. "*Warum lasst ihr mich nicht über die Klinge springen?*" [Why don't you put me to the sword?], he asked. I sat with Eric in one of the interrogations; he laughed at Eric and mocked the British Intelligence Service. At the Nuremberg trials a year later, he was sentenced to life in prison, but his Italian partners smuggled him out of prison a few years later. His right-hand man, Erich Priebke, managed to flee and lived under a false name for 50 years in southern Argentina.

I had already lived through many milestones in my short life: escaping Germany, kibbutz life, the battles in Africa and Italy, and now a new one: I had fallen in love with Claudia. I had had some short affairs before, but this one was explosive. Claudia was the reason I constantly returned to Rome.

I had fallen in love with Claudia, but also with Rome, with its wonderful sepia-colored streetscapes, its piazzas of all shapes and sizes, the old buildings breathing history, the theaters and concerts, and the artsy Via Margutta. I became addicted to Rome's sophisticated air. Rome had always been a cultured city, and the end of the war in Italy only elevated its magnificent style. The cultural events that had been advertised in Italian and German before, were now advertised in Italian and English.

The end of the war also opened new educational opportunities. Many courses were offered in convenient evening classes for the thousands of discharged Italian soldiers who had interrupted their studies when the war started. I decided to look for some class for myself. Growing up in Berlin I had dreamed of becoming an architect like my Uncle Fritz, who was part of the Bauhaus group in Berlin. But I had never had an opportunity to do so, as I had had to escape Germany before finishing high school. Maybe I could enroll in a design course for war returnees? I looked for a class, introduced myself, and was accepted without further questions. Who would dare question the abilities of an Allied officer? My Italian classmates enjoyed the unusual spectacle of a student in British uniform, applying himself to learn to draw and to handle ink pens, tracing paper, and a drawing rule. I was an oddity, no doubt, but I felt fabulously good.

I had found my passion. At that moment I made the decision not to return to the kibbutz after the war.

Claudia and I explored Rome from end to end. I got to know this wonderful city like the back of my hand. Sometimes we dined in restaurants, enjoying delicious Italian specialties, a luxury compared with my British military food. But mostly, we sat in the cafés. We sat in elegant cafés on the Via Veneto, where Rome's elites gathered to see and be seen; we sat in the popular cafés on the Piazza Navona, with its incomparable silhouette and baroque water fountains; we sat in the British Tea Room at the Piazza di Spagna, famous for hosting Lord Byron, Stendhal, and other famed writers; we sat at the Caffè Greco on Via Condotti, frequented by the bohemian crowd. I never tired of observing and breathing in this beautiful city.

I was a newly rich man spending the money we had collected from the Italian prisoners at the end of the battle of Anzio. For the first time in my life, I enjoyed some small luxuries. But I was also a careful planner and placed a large part of my military salary in the new savings account offered by the British Army for the postwar period.

In the Caffè Greco everything was antique: the tables, the chairs, the bar; the mirrors, with their patina of past splendors. The walls were covered with paintings and sketches by artists of yesteryear who had paid their bills with their work. Claudia and I sat in the Caffè Greco countless times looking into each other's eyes in reciprocal love. But we also watched the guests, while Claudia whispered in my ear who was who and filled me on the inexhaustible gossip. I became a regular, sipping my favorite drink, a semi-dry martini.

Claudia discovered that the café had a sign-in book for famous guests. I asked our waiter about it, and he pointed to half a dozen bound volumes sitting in a glass case. Since I was a familiar face, he brought me two volumes, pointing out the notes written by some famous people. I then asked for the most recent volume. He did not like my request but brought it anyway. There, I saw the notes by German officers with their signatures. The last inscription was dated only a month before my arrival to Rome. The waiter was relieved when I did not make any comment, but when I indicated that I would sign my own name and title into this volume, he decided he needed authorization. But who would deny this request to a British soldier if he had not denied it to the occupiers? I evened history: I signed my name and my greetings in English and Hebrew in the 1944 yearbook.

Many other historic moments cast their light and their shadows on my life. On June 6, 1944, I woke up and went to the kitchen for coffee. Everybody had gathered around the radio and was talking agitatedly. It was D-Day. At dawn the Allies had landed in Normandy, France, and opened a third front in the war. The Germans now faced great resistance on the Russian, the Italian, and the French fronts. By now, nobody doubted that the Allies would win the war. For three years the Allies had lost most battles and most campaigns, but they had not lost the war. Three crucial battles had changed the weight and the pace of the war: the Battle of Britain, impeding the German invasion in 1940–1941, the Battle of Stalingrad on the Russian front in 1942, and the Battle of El Alamein in Africa, also in 1942. Three years of continuous defeats did not translate into a lost war for the Allies, but one and a half years of German losses sealed their war defeat.

The Allies' eventual success became palpable on D-Day. No one, however, could foresee the details ahead. How quickly would the end come? How much more human sacrifice and physical destruction would it take to reach the end? How much longer would the German Army endure?

At the end of July 1944, an assassination attempt against Hitler triggered a deep and ruthless internal purge within the German Army, whose leaders pushed to total war: no mercy, lack of any sensible thinking. We witnessed the real meaning of the German term *Kadavergehorsamkeit*: blind obedience, annulment of any reflective will or self-questioning, emptying of the essence of life. This was what our troops now encountered on the front lines.

There was another aspect at play as well: your fighting determination increases as the distance between your back and your own home shortens. The battles of El Alamein, Tobruk, and Sidi Barani in Africa were crucial, and both sides wanted to win. But they were fought on foreign land. Neither side, German nor British, had a deep attachment to or affection for those desert oases. But here in Italy, it was a different war. Each German defeat shortened the distance to the symbolic and real boundary against which the Germans were being pushed back: their own Alps, the boundary of their own beloved land.

There were changes on our side too. The tactical military intelligence that I had worked on, now turned to strategic intelligence. And even though we were military intelligence, little by little our work also slipped into political intelligence. The central question among our leaders was no longer how to win the war but what kind of peace could be achieved. What pieces of land

and what quotas of power would each party capture for their side? There were also the first glimpses of electronic espionage.

For three months I lived in wonderful Rome. For three months I enjoyed fabulous love, fascinating design classes, great culture, and interesting work. And then I felt a restlessness, an itching to return to adventure. So when two special missions were scheduled in Pisa and Florence, I volunteered to go. Claudia was desolate. I lied and told her I had been assigned to this mission; I assured her I would return alive, and I did.

Four months later I was called again to a mission in Greece. I recalled the stories about the Acropolis, the oracles, and the Olympian gods that I had learned in school. I wanted to see these places, and I raised my hand again to volunteer.

On my Matchless motorbike. Over 80,000 Matchless G3 / G3L models
were used by the British Army during the war.

WITH THE PARTISANS

GREECE, 1944

Kiss me again, beloved.
Clean that gun, comrade.
Pablo Neruda, *The Soldier's Love*

Our unit of 14 men, under the command of Major Clutterbuck, boarded a plane to Greece with a stopover in Bari, Italy, where we were briefed by General Sir Harold Macmillan, Churchill's minister and protégé, who had also briefed us eight months earlier at the gates of Rome. General Macmillan explained our mission. The Greek Partisans were collaborating with the Allies in liberating Greece from Axis occupation, but they had no experience in handling prisoners of war. We, the British Intelligence Service, would take on this task. We would form small units to move with the Partisans in action and assist with prisoners. But most importantly, we were entrusted with a parallel mission: to observe and discover the presence of Russian agents among the Partisans – who were linked to the Greek Communist Party.

As the Germans retreated, the Greek political division deepened over the struggle for power, pushing the country to a potential civil war. On the one hand were the communist-led Partisans, and on the other, the Realists, who favored the return of former King George II. Greece's postwar political make up became the focus of covert opposition between the British and the Russians. British intelligence was now directed in large measure at obtaining information of a political rather than a military nature. And we were now going straight into this conflict.

We flew across the Adriatic Sea and landed near Athens, to head to northern Greece. My field unit was composed of four officers, a driver, and a truck full of supplies. After a long journey through a rugged and desolate landscape, we arrived at our destination: a small village with a handful of stone houses that so blended into their surroundings as to be almost invisible to an untrained eye. We lodged in one of the houses, with a single room, two rickety wooden doors, no windows, and a dirt floor. Water was drawn from a well located beyond the cluster of houses. The latrine was past the houses in the opposite direction. We shook hands with the villagers; they shared their wine with us, and we shared our beer.

It began to get dark. The village had no electricity and there were no candles. The villagers were familiar with their surroundings and moved easily between the stones in the dark. We, however, did not. We had a battery-powered flashlight but not enough batteries to last for several nights. It all became more complicated the next day. The village men discussed plans, but we did not speak Greek and they spoke nothing but Greek. Pantomime, hand gestures, and drawings on the ground helped somewhat. After hours of attempts to communicate by all possible means, we were able to get some basic information: they knew where the German troops were; there were no Italians; they planned to surround them, capture them, and bring them to the village. Could we join them? No. What should we do? Wait. For how long? Shrugs.

We looked at the Partisan villagers. Simple, robust, healthy, and confident people wearing old and ragged clothes. "Weapons?" we asked. Shrugs again. We suggested building corrals for the prisoners. The villagers signaled to us the futility of this but helped collect logs, stones, and thorny bushes to form a fence. The fence was precarious, but these were the only materials available in the village. There was not an inch of wire or any manufactured supplies. How many Germans did they think there were in the region? Shrugs. Were there other groups of Partisans in the vicinity? Yes. How many? Shrugs again.

There was no action that day. At sunset, the village men started to put on shoes. Silhouettes of old rifles and shotguns emerged in the shadows; leather canteens were filled with some concoction; and then, without farewells, the men silently disappeared into the darkness. The few women remained in the village and retreated to their homes. There was nothing for us to do but wait.

As the first rays of morning light crept over the rocky hills, the village women started to talk in agitated voices. They pointed in one direction with their hands, calling us. We strained our eyes to see at the distant landscape. Yes, far out on the mountain, about 500 meters from our village, a dark mass was moving slowly. Sheep? People? As the day dawned, the view became clearer. A mass of bodies was moving slowly at ground level, on four legs. A few moved on two legs, human beings. Unbelievable. About 400 German soldiers were slowly crawling on their hands and feet across the thorny, stone-covered hillside, driven from behind like a herd by 50 Partisans, as if they were their animals. Most of the German soldiers wore their uniforms and steel helmets, but about 50 of them wore no shoes, jackets, or helmets. The Partisans wore those, proudly.

The Partisans made the men crawl all the way down to the village. Then they lined them up in five rows and stripped them of their rifles, jackets, pants, socks, and shoes, until they were in their underwear, "for mercy and morals," as explained by the Partisan spokesman. Once all were stripped, the Partisans handed us the prisoners. Their part of the work was completed.

They had done a very good job. Under such conditions, nobody could have done it better. "Do you feel any compassion?" I asked the spokesman. "Would the Germans have had compassion on us?" he said. "They would have crushed us for information and then killed us. We do not kill. Did we take their clothes? Yes, we are ragged, as you see. Now we can dress ourselves and our comrades. It's time for the fascists to suffer. Feed them? That is your problem; you, the British, wanted to have them. Good luck."

A total of 3,000 German soldiers, now prisoners, were our responsibility.

The German prisoners crawled willingly into our corrals. They would not dream of escaping. Where to? And who would want to escape the good fortune of having survived the war and being a prisoner of the British? They would now receive water and an "iron ration," a large, compact piece of protein and chocolate that feeds a person for four days and takes hunger away.

There was no need for interrogations. The Germans were withdrawing from Greece and these prisoners were the "rear guard" responsible for keeping the Partisans at bay to protect the retreat of the German leaders. In war, the rear guard is the sacrificial lamb, a planned military cost. These soldiers had not expected to come out alive. This rear guard was a *Strafbataillon*, a penal battalion, as they existed in the German Army, composed of men who had a tainted military history, had received a sentence for their political inclinations, or were criminals. In these *Strafbataillons* the Germans designated the criminals as commanders, and the politically sentenced as members of the troop. The *Strafbataillons* were then placed in the riskiest positions. There was probably more than one anti-Nazi among them. But the ups and downs of war, and the arbitrary distribution of trench sides and uniforms, did not allow one to recognize sympathizers.

Meanwhile, the Germans' weapons had vanished. The Partisans had hidden them and delivered to us old weapons instead, to comply with the international "Disarmament Agreement." It was a crude mockery, but we sympathized with these men and chose to ignore the whereabouts of the weapons. They were probably assigned to ELAS, the Greek People's Liberation Army, the largest armed guerrilla force in Greece during Nazi occupation. ELAS had actively collaborated with the British, but as the Nazis retreated, this collaboration eroded and evolved into mutual mistrust, since the British backed the former Greek King George in exile, whom the Partisans strongly opposed.

This was the very first time in my military career that I was faced with a decision between conscience and total obedience. It took me by surprise, and it made me reflect, but I did not doubt. I did not know then that this would not be the only time, just the first one. The war was about to end, and peace was about to arrive; every action and decision was now less about military strategy and more about political interests. New political war fronts were emerging.

I was assigned to two other similar missions in Greece. In the last one, 15,000 Italian soldiers surrendered. The British Army's goal was to repatriate them back to Italy as soon as possible, to avoid imprisoning and feeding people who were no longer a danger. But the British also wanted to identify and retain the true fascists within this mass of prisoners. This was our mission, and we were given only seven days to accomplish it. How could the four of us manage to question 15,000 prisoners to discover the hardcore Nazis among them? "That's your problem; solve it."

We knew we only had to interrogate the officers, but there were 4,000 officers among the prisoners. How would we do this? Our team leader, a bright Maltese, saved the situation. "We'll do this in four days," he said, "because I need three days to be with my lover. I know how to tackle this challenge. We know that only hardline fascist party members were granted free weekends, so we will simply ask each officer about his weekend adventures." Brilliant: I would have never thought of this.

We formed two corrals and lined up the officers for questioning. "How were your weekends? What can you tell me about Greek women?" Long face, drooping shoulders: "Bad, sergeant, no time, no money." "Go to the corral on the right." Next one: "How were your weekends? How are the Greek women, man?" "Wonderful, fiery, my sergeant." "Go to the corral on the left." The men's long or bright faces were often enough response. In four days, we completed our mission.

We now had three days off before reporting back. The Maltese lieutenant vanished and so did my companions. What would I do? I called Temi. I had met Temi on my arrival in Greece; she was the ELAS spokesperson and had impressed me greatly. She had the classical Greek profile that I had seen in the marvelous ancient Greek bas-reliefs in my history schoolbooks: a single straight line from her forehead to the tip of her nose. I was fascinated with this beautiful feature. Temi was bright and cultured, spoke several languages, and passionately defended the Partisans. I called her and I asked if she had some time to show me the marvels of her culture.

For two days Temi and I toured the Acropolis and the classical and Byzantine marvels in Athens. Temi shared her knowledge and love for classical architecture, and its perfect dimensions. And at night she shared with me her own charms. She was a wonderful teacher, and I was a willing student. Time passed fast, and I reported back to duty in Italy.

LILI MARLEEN

ITALY, 1945

And there 'neath that far off lantern light,
I'd hold you tight.
We'd kiss goodnight,
my Lili of the lamplight.
"Lili Marleen," a popular WWII love song

A letter to my friend Bobby, 2005:

Bobby, do you remember May 8, 1945, the day the Nazis surrendered?
We were entrenched looking north towards the German border. There
had been no shooting or combat for the last 60 hours. We were all
waiting, waiting. And then, from behind the lines, a murmur rippled
across our trenches, rising up like a wave coming towards us: "It's over!
It's over!"

Magical, intoxicating words. We jumped out of the trenches, we
threw our rifles in the air, we trampled the earth and shouted: "It's all
over, it's over!"

To our right, the Italian soldiers stepped out of their trenches crying:
"Pace, pace, è finita la guerra!" In front of us, the German soldiers
shouted: "Schluss, Ende!" We did not mix, we did not hug, we did not
shake hands. But we all felt the same emotion, the same relief. Tens of

thousands of soldiers celebrated the end of the nightmare of war. Once the shouting was exhausted, a great silence set in. A voice started to sing "Lili Marleen" and we all joined in – the British, the Italians, the Germans. One shared song, all voices in unison.

The British anthem was sung standing; the traditional British Army song "It's a long way to Tipperary" was always sung marching; but "Lili Marleen," the most popular love song among soldiers on both fronts of the war, was sung sitting. Do you remember the song, Bobby? We sang it so many times across Africa and Italy; it became part of all armies' repertoire, transmitted across combat lines and enemy borders. "Lili Marleen" is the story of a young woman who says goodbye to her lover who goes to war. She longs for his presence and waits for his return, standing under a lantern. The romantic melody was loved by all soldiers; it represented what we all longed for, what we all dreamt of while sitting in the war trenches for years.

I looked at the rough men that I had led for the past 14 months of battle across Italy. They sat with their heads down, hiding their tears. "Men don't cry", we were taught as children. "Hart wie Stahl" [Tough as steel], was the motto in the German Army. "Save your emotions" was the instruction in the British Army.

I looked up at the dark night sky, searching for the Milky Way, that bright cloud of stars. Perhaps I saw there the reflection of the lantern under which my own Lili Marleen might be waiting for me. Our longing for the love left behind became at that moment a dream for our future. Now the return to home would become a reality and our Lili Marleen would there for us. Yes, Lili Marleen belonged to everyone. Each and every soldier in this war had his own Lili Marleen.

I also had my Lili Marleen: shiny black hair, blue eyes, a soft, tender voice. It was four years since I had kissed Lotti for the last time in the kibbutz, when I left to join the army. Those were tough times, lacking communication or news. When I returned home, she had married someone else.

We survived; we returned home; we found new love; we formed wonderful families; we raised children and grandchildren. We are grateful; we were the lucky ones.

A toast to life, "L'chaim!" [To life!].

Heidrich (Lt), son of General
                    and partisan.
VIETINGHOFF. C in C. ——————.
WOLFF   c. in c. SS ITALY.
Mr and Mrs HIMMLER.
"Axis Sally"
ROSSETTI.
Kappler (Fosse Ardeatine, Rom.)
Uebeweiler, Rainer (Gauleiter).
Kroullert (Süd-Ost Europa. MUFTI)
Prince Borghese

Page from my War Diary, recording the names of our high-level
prisoners: On this page: Heidrich, Wolff, Kappler, Prince Borghese, Axis
Sally, Mrs. Himmler.

SURRENDER OF THE LEADERS

ITALY, 1945

In front of us, flames.
In the air that smell of burning flesh.
Elie Wiesel, *Night*

What a pleasure it was to be back in Rome! Claudia enveloped me with kisses; my design classmates greeted me with affectionate hugs.

The air was charged with news. The German and Italian armies were collapsing on the north front. The war was about to end. We now had to prepare for the German and Italian surrender and ensure that this did not turn into chaos. My unit was moved to Florence and divided into three groups to take charge of the surrendering high-ranking officials: Bobby led the German unit, Eric the civilian unit, and I the Italian unit.

My friend Jerry reappeared after a long absence. Jerry was a German-born American soldier. He had left Germany for the United States as soon as Hitler was elected and went on to study journalism. When the war broke out, he enlisted as a war correspondent for the *Stars and Stripes*, the US Army newspaper. I had first met Jerry during the landing in Anzio and allowed him to interview our German and Italian prisoners. His article was a journalistic success, and he revisited me every now and then to share news and to seek new information. He had a keen instinct for burning news and knew how to find me in the vast sea of the British Army.

This time he said, "Rudi, ask for a few days off and come with me. I am going with an American military detachment to report as they liberate the Dachau concentration camp. Come, jump into my jeep." I reflected. "No, partner, I can't leave; everyone is needed right now here; and I don't think I can stomach what you will see." Jerry returned three weeks later and handed me his photographs. "The smell of burnt flesh," he said. "I will never forget. It hung over the camp like a fog of death. The enormity of bodies piled up like logs helter-skelter. I prayed the Kaddish for the dead." Jerry's images sickened me; even today, they are more than I can bear.

The scent of the war's end was in the air. There was no combat anymore; both sides just maintained their positions. Why fight to gain more ground at this point? Nobody wanted to die in the last days of war, when peace was on the horizon. Everyone wanted to return home safely.

Emissaries from the Italian Army under the command of Field Marshal Rodolfo Graziani, loyal to German fascists, showed up with a white flag to negotiate an unconditional but dignified surrender. Graziani was the last Italian marshal to remain loyal to Mussolini. The Italian fascist dictator had fled north, where he was captured and shot by the Italian Partisans in April of 1945. Graziani held out for four more days and then surrendered in May 1945.

The Allied command agreed to his surrender. After negotiating the terms, the surrender document was penned in English, and we translated it into Italian and hand-delivered it to the Italian emissaries. All details of the formal surrender were agreed: place, day, time, procedure, participants, and much more. Dignity was now assured.

I oversaw the preparations for this historic surrender ceremony. I was nervous; I never imagined that I would be so close to such events. On the day of the surrender, everything was ready. I had chosen a wide-open field. At one end of the field we set up a long table on easels, covered with a white tablecloth, and on top, the official documents for signature. It was nine-thirty in the morning, the agreed time for the ceremony. Standing by the table were the highest-ranking Allied officers, journalists, and photographers. My team and I stood discreetly further back. We all waited.

The Italians were nowhere in sight. My watch ticked on, to ten o'clock. The expectant silence now turned into a low murmur. Had the Italians changed their mind? Or was this just the Italian informality? Finally, at ten-thirty, the Italians appeared at the end of the field, wearing their uniforms with their stripes and badges. Field Marshal Graziani could be identified from afar for his stature; he was nearly two meters tall. The ceremony proceeded exactly as planned. The documents were signed, and the surrender was symbolically sealed with a handshake – that of the international brotherhood of militarism and war machine.

Everything was over. The Italian general was now our prisoner of war.

It was my responsibility to follow up. Some of my men cut across the field to take charge of the Italian troops. My partner and I approached Graziani and guided him to our jeep to take him to our headquarters in Florence. We had all been up since early dawn in this intensely emotional day, and thirst and hunger were noticeable now. Our assistant had left a canteen with tea and two sandwiches in our jeep. "Signore Maresciallo, do you want to share this snack with us?" we asked. He answered without hesitation: "*Si, con piacere*" [Yes, my pleasure.] The three of us shared our food.

We drove Graziani to Florence, to our unit's high-ranking prisoners' quarters: a large villa on the elegant Michelangelo Avenue that curled up the hill to Piazalle Michelangelo, where one could enjoy the best views over this magnificent city.

A couple hours after we arrived, my friend Bobby arrived in his jeep with his high-ranking prisoners from Germany. A large man descended, dressed in a black uniform and a cap bearing the skull and crossbones, the insignia of the SS. "General Wolff," whispered Bobby, "SS chief and brains of the German southern front." Wolff stood erect, with a half-cynical and half-conciliatory smile. He had contacted the Allies to negotiate his surrender a week before his partners in Berlin. He knew everything was lost and wanted to be seen as a conciliator. This war criminal, a disgusting being, wanted to save his skin and he knew how to do it.

The following day Eric arrived from Switzerland with two women. "Frau Himmler and her daughter," he said. Heinrich Himmler was the ruthless top leader of the SS and the Gestapo, the powerful agencies for security, surveillance, and terror in Nazi Germany and Nazi-occupied Europe. The SS enforced the Nazi racial policy and ran the concentration and extermination camps. The Gestapo operated under the SS umbrella to detect Nazi enemies and police people on their commitment to Nazi ideology. The SS was responsible for the killing of six million Jews and millions of others in the Holocaust. And this butcher had hidden his family in Switzerland.

More and more prisoners were brought in, and soon all the villa's rooms were occupied. Bobby and I were then commissioned to transport some prisoners to Rome, where we arrived on May 8, 1945 – the day Nazi Germany finally surrendered unconditionally.

VE-Day: Victory in Europe Day.

Every activity was put on hold across Rome and Europe. Everybody was chanting, hugging, and dancing. The war in Europe was finally over, after five and a half long and painful years. This was the day everybody had dreamed of; this was the most desired day.

Our old rooms at Pensione Elguetta in Piazza del Gesù were no longer available. Bobby and I could not find a room anywhere in Rome at all. So, we set up our military tent in the Pensione's yard to spend the night. What an irony: on this very first night of peace, we were back to sleeping in our war tent. Bobby began preparing to sleep. We were both exhausted, but I couldn't rest now.

"How can you go to sleep, Bobby, on this night of victory?" I asked my friend. "How can you sleep in this crowning moment of our young lives? Come, let's celebrate with everybody else." "You go, Rudi; leave me alone," Bobby grunted as he fell onto his blanket on the ground. Although exhausted and hungry, I joined the celebrations. People embraced me and offered me drinks – wine and whiskey. I was not a drinker, but this was truly a unique occasion. My resistance was low, and I got very drunk for the first time in my life. I missed Bobby, my best friend and war mate, and decided to look for him. He cursed me for waking him up. "Bobby, you cannot sleep now," I said. "Yes, I can." "No," I insisted, "you will not." And in my drunkenness, I took a match and put our tent on fire to force him up. Everything burned.

VE-Day! The party lasted 40 hours. It was not much, compared with five and a half years of war and destruction. We celebrated victory, but we also celebrated having survived. And this was not a result of personal merit; it was, above all, great, great luck.

Yes, the party lasted days. But for us Jews, a new heartbreak was beginning. We were now facing the reality of what until that moment had been only rumors: the gas chambers, the mass murders, the genocide of our people.

Who had survived and who had perished? Who was alive? Where? Who had been killed? The concentration camps' lists of prisoners were slowly released, one after the other, as the Allies took over the camps; the horrific reality of the Holocaust was unraveled and fully revealed. With each new list, week by week, the number of victims increased. If the previous figure had seemed incomprehensible, unimaginable, it was still not enough. The numbers continued to increase.

Six million dead Jews.

Berlin in ruins, 1945.

RETURN TO BERLIN
ROME TO BERLIN, 1945

What is history?
History is written by the victors.
Author unknown

Little by little we learned about the real tragedy of the Nazi concentration camps and the magnitude of the Jewish death toll. First we heard rumors through soldiers who joined our unit from other European war fronts. Then we heard it from soldiers who were returning from Dachau with photographs of what they had seen. But only after VE-Day did we learn the real magnitude of the tragedy, the number of camps, the number of deaths, and the horrors of the crematoria. The reality of it was tremendous.

And then, in addition to the dead, there were a million concentration camp survivors, those who were on the verge of death when the Red Army liberated the camps in Eastern Europe. A Jewish-American newspaper began to publish lists of survivors, as they were slowly identified through censuses. Columns of names in tiny print were published week after week, for months, and for years. All Jews around the world read those lists, week after week, month after month, hoping to find the name of a loved one, of a friend, a classmate, or a neighbor. We read the lists three times; first eagerly and hopeful to find a name; then again, more carefully to scan deeper; and then a third time, very slowly, to ensure we had not missed the name we had not found.

At that time, I received a letter from my father letting me know that his brother, my Onkel Fritz, had survived the Terezín concentration camp in Czechoslovakia, liberated by the Soviet troops on May 8, 1945. The news filled me with strong emotions, as I sensed my father's anguish about his brother and the fate of the rest of our family.

My good son: Today we received a telegram from your Onkel Fritz. He is alive. He was deported in March 1943 to Terezín Concentration Camp and is still there. Please, try to contact him and send him what he needs most urgently. Our letters cannot reach him, but you, in Europe, may have a better chance to contact him. What challenges he must have confronted and suffered! And the anguish for his wife... Forget we never will; but we can draw a line at the end of this terrible war and recommence our lives. Dear son, please help Onkel Fritz. Your Vati.

These were uncle Fritz's words to my father:

May this letter arrive to its destination. I hope you are all alive. Now, this terrible war has finally come to an end. All that we loved and valued is destroyed ... and we must now recover from our deep wounds and repair our torn lives. I am totally alone.

Since March 1943 I have been interned in Terezín, violently uprooted from everything and everybody I love. Comparatively, I did not fare that badly within the walls of this prison at the edge of the river Elbe, as I was assigned to run an old brewery. Food was very scarce or non-existent. Only now, since the Russians arrived, do we have enough to eat. Whether Berthe, my wife, is still alive, I don't know. In Berlin they tore us apart. We were taken on the same day, Berthe, from her workplace, and me, from home, and I never saw her nor heard from her again. I do know she was sent to Auschwitz, and from there, there is no return... Maybe some miraculous star has kept her alive so I may see her again... My brother-in-law and my nephews were also deported to

I approached my commander, Colonel Roberts, and asked him for time off to look for my Uncle Fritz. He was a cultured man who appreciated our work. We had contributed to making his unit one of great prestige, which had garnered him medals, promotions, and authority. Now he showed his appreciation: "Yes, sergeant," he said. "I'll give you 28 days of compassionate leave. Make sure you return on time. If you do not, I would have to declare you a deserter."

I planned out my trip. One of my companions had just returned from Hungary and reported on what he had seen. We listened in horror and disbelief. He said to me, "Rudi, do not go to Terezín. The Soviets are moving all survivors to their place of origin. By the time you arrive, they will have closed the concentration camp. Your uncle will surely be sent to Berlin; go there to look for him."

In those early postwar days, Berlin was under the authority of the Allied North Atlantic Command. My unit was part of the Allied Central Mediterranean Command with jurisdiction up to the German border. I would need help to enter Berlin. I asked Colonel Roberts for two items; a Service Commission addressed to Berlin, and an Intelligence Service envelope with our royal seal, "On His Majesty's Service." I then filled two large backpacks with food and clothes and departed.

There was no air travel available at all. I knew the journey would be long, but I never imagined how complicated it would actually be. First, I traveled from Naples, Italy, to Vienna, Austria, on a military train that was transporting huge numbers of troops in both directions. It was slow and very uncomfortable, but I managed to get to Vienna. There, I learned that there was a newly established civilian rail service to Munich, Germany, running every other day, to help address the immense challenge of moving thousands of refugees and displaced people throughout Europe. Millions of people were trying to get to somewhere different from where they were.

I learned that this new rail service had a coach for Allied troops and decided to get a seat on this train. I arrived at the train station at dawn but could hardly access the platform. Hundreds and hundreds of people were already there waiting for the train, dressed in thick clothes, warm hats, gloves, a backpack, and a rope on their shoulders. The train finally arrived after an hour's delay. But the coaches were invisible under a huge human mass that hung out from the windows and doors. If a regular coach carried 180 people, this train carried 280 people packed inside each coach plus 120 hanging outside. This was why everybody carried a rope and warm clothing: they tied themselves to the window frames and traveled hanging out in the open. And what did the hundreds of people on the Vienna station platform do? They formed a second layer, tied to those already tied to the train. A compact human mass enveloped the train's sides and roof. No wonder the train was so slow: the process of people tying themselves to the train took quite some time.

Somehow, I managed to climb onto the military coach. The train departed and crossed the Alps through tunnels. No more people were allowed to tie themselves onto the train, as it had happened before that the hanging human mass had been crushed in the narrow space within the tunnel walls.

We traveled for endless hours across Austria to the German border, where suddenly, all the hanging human mass abandoned the train. What had happened? All those traveling on the packed train lacked documentation to legally cross into Germany, so they got off the train at the border and crossed the Alps clandestinely on foot with smugglers, getting back onto the train on the German side. This illegal traffic functioned in a very organized manner, and thousands of people resorted to this train-march-train strategy.

The few lucky ones who had proper documents stayed on the train. The military border police checked all documents carefully and took off the train those who carried false documents. Once we crossed into Germany the train stopped at the first station, and the great avalanche of people who had crossed the border on foot, climbed back onto the train, tying themselves onto doors and windows again. Eventually, the packed train arrived in Munich, 22 hours after leaving Vienna. I was the only passenger on the military coach.

In Munich, however, I learned that there was no transport of any kind from Munich to Berlin. Another big setback.

The Allied powers – the United States, the United Kingdom, France, and the Soviet Union – now controlled Germany, which they had divided into four occupation zones. The Soviets tightly controlled Eastern Germany, where Berlin was located, while the Americans, British, and French controlled the rest. I learned that the Soviets had opened one single corridor connecting the American zone to Berlin, across the Soviet zone. This corridor started in Frankfurt and was exclusively for a military train. So, I left Munich to Frankfurt, traveling in another train overloaded with people.

The displaced people in Europe numbered millions. The very few functioning trains were the only means of transportation besides walking. There were over ten million German-speaking refugees or ex-prisoners in Central and Eastern Europe who were now moving back to Germany. In Germany there were some eight million foreign people, mainly forced laborers and prisoners, plus 400,000 survivors from concentration camps, who were trying to get out of Germany and back to their countries of origin. The largest population migration in all of European history was taking place at that moment. And thousands and thousands of these displaced people resorted to walking. For weeks and weeks, months and months, people walked and walked, covering up to 700 kilometers to reach their destinations.

In Frankfurt, the station chief informed me that there was indeed an American military train running from Frankfurt to Berlin, and that spaces on this train were handled directly by the US Army. I immediately went to the US Army office, and stood in a long line, patiently waiting for my turn. The attending soldier checked my documents and said, "Sergeant, you can take the train in three days. I will put you on the waiting list." "But I must travel today," I said. "Impossible," he responded. I despaired. "Listen, mate, I am traveling in search of the only survivor in my family. My permit is very limited; I have been traveling for days and days, and at this rate I will not be able to reach him on time. Give me a hand and help me get onto the train." He listened impassively. "I'm sorry, these are the rules; come back in three days."

I stepped aside; I was desperate. As I sorted my papers, I looked up and it seemed to me that one of the soldiers behind the counter was subtly winking at me. I decided to wait. At six o'clock sharp, the office closed, and the soldiers left. The one who had winked at me, approached me: "I heard your story, I am also a Jew. Let me see your papers, maybe I can give you a hand." He looked at them intently. "Your papers should state your right to priority. Without it, the official has no choice but to deny your request. Look, here in your Special Pass there is a space; use it for the annotation you need." He said goodbye and left.

Great tip, but how to execute it? All of Frankfurt had closed for the day. I walked through the deserted streets; suddenly, I saw a US Army 24-hour first-aid office. I stepped in and asked if they had a typewriter that I could borrow. "Of course," said the young man, with typical American generosity. The typewriter's typography was not identical to the one on my documents, but I hoped nobody would notice. I placed my document in the typewriter's slot and carefully typed in the magical phrase. I then thanked the soldier and left. The next day, I showed up again at the US Army office and stood in line again, making sure that my line's attending officer was not the same one as yesterday's. I presented my documents; the official checked them and said, "Here is your ticket for tonight's train." What a joy! I wanted to hug the soldier who had helped me the previous night, but I kept my composure. I looked in his direction, he looked up, and I thanked him with my eyes.

I boarded the military train that same night. It was a sealed non-stop train and noticeably different from the trains I had traveled on previously: it was well heated and carried no standing passengers. We passed through station after station along the way without stopping. Through my window I could see the platforms packed with people waiting for an opportunity to get on a train. We entered Berlin's Soviet sector at night, after passing two checkpoints. Berlin was now a divided city, one part Soviet, one part British - American. Finally, at dawn the next morning, we entered the American sector of Berlin. It had taken me more than a full week to travel from Rome to Berlin.

It was seven years since I had left Germany as a refugee teenager, and now I was returning as a victorious soldier. What a reversal of roles and of fortune!

I stepped out of the train station and looked around. I recognized the neighborhood, in the Zehlendorf district, at the rim of the Grunewald Forest. The district had been developed in 1928 and became famous for its modern design, which broke with Berlin's traditional pattern of urban blocks and brick buildings. Instead, this district featured free forms in the "Garden City" style and buildings with flat roofs and daring colors. People would visit the neighborhood either to admire or to be shocked by it. Its lead designer, Bruno Taut, formed part of the Bauhaus, the avant-garde German design movement which my Uncle Fritz was part of, and which the Nazis had banned. How symbolic that I would enter Berlin precisely here, as I returned to look for my Uncle Fritz.

I took the U-Bahn, Berlin's subway, which had been partially restored, to the Bayrisher Platz station near my uncle's former home. I emerged up in the center of the Bayrisher Platz, the square that I had frequented so often during my childhood. At first glance it seemed unchanged, but then I realized that the facades around it were just ghost silhouettes; there were no buildings behind. Berlin had been bombed intensely and was heavily damaged. The solid brick facades had survived, but I could see the sky through the empty window openings.

It was ten in the morning. The sky was gray, and few people walked on the street. I sat on a bench to reflect on the meeting with my Uncle Fritz. Less than 100 meters from where I sat was his former apartment, Salzburgerstrasse #11. Was the building still there? Would my uncle be there or not? What would he look like? My mind was full of questions. I had not had a calm moment to meditate on this before. During the eight days of travel my attention had been totally focused on advancing against time and overcoming the innumerable obstacles I had faced. I now took a deep breath.

I saw a boy crossing the square and I called to him in German. He approached me, surprised and scared to be questioned by an English officer in perfect German. "Do you want a cigarette?" I asked him. "Of course." "Then, go to Salzburgerstrasse #11 and check if the building still exists, whether it is inhabited, and if there is someone there with the surname Haymann." The boy ran to perform his task and soon returned: "Yes, the building is there; there are four name signs on the left side and one of them is Haymann." "Do you want to earn a second cigarette? Go back, ring the bell, ask for Mr. Haymann, and tell him that his nephew Rudi will come to see him in 20 minutes."

Twenty minutes. I estimated that would give my uncle enough time to recover from the surprise, but not so much that it would become an unbearable wait. The boy returned. "I rang the bell. A lady opened and said that Mr. Haymann is not in at this moment." I thanked the boy and gave him his well-earned cigarettes.

I grabbed my two backpacks and walked to my uncle's apartment and rang the bell. A gray-faced lady opened the door just a crack, and grimaced when she saw a soldier in British uniform. I spoke to her in German and carefully explained that I was Mr. Haymann's nephew, and that I came from far away to visit him without warning. As she listened to my words, she opened the door a little bit more and then invited me in. She pointed to the two rooms in which my Uncle Fritz now lived. She told me that my uncle had recently started to work part-time at the School of Architecture at the Free University of Berlin; he would be back at five in the afternoon. I left my two backpacks in my uncle's room, thanked the lady, and left.

Now, I just had to wait.

Uncle Fritz as a German soldier in World War I.

UNCLE FRITZ

BERLIN, 1945

The only truly dead
are only those who have been forgotten.
Old Jewish proverb

I had six hours to wait. I set out to explore Berlin, my hometown, the city I had left as a teenager seven years before, fleeing Nazi persecution. Strangely, the dates of my departure and of my return coincided almost exactly.

I walked silently through the streets of my childhood. A stark testimony of war, they were framed by facades with gaping empty windows. Roofless buildings were open to the sky, like faces with hollowed eyes, decapitated bodies. Millions of cubic meters of debris were piled up on streets and sidewalks.

The day was cold and gray. There were no vehicles at all. I walked in the center of the street to observe both facades at the same time. The few people whose paths I crossed, walked fast, minding their business. Nobody strolled; there was nothing to see, nothing to buy, nowhere to gather.

I reached the Ku'damm, once Berlin's most elegant avenue, lined with shops and cafés. It was now a gray, sad street. The former large store windows were boarded up with wooden planks. Glass was the scarcest material after the war. A few stores had a small, irregular piece of glass the size of a postcard embedded in the wooden planks, to allow a view of what was inside. I got closer to peek through these peepholes. Random objects were displayed: used furniture, clothing, used shoes, tools, construction materials. Nothing had a price, nothing was for sale, but everything was available for trade: a dining room table in exchange for a woman's coat, shoes for glass, a carpet for a lockable door.

As I advanced towards the zoo, I saw more activity; the streetcar was running, black-market vendors were hanging around, and off-duty soldiers were looking for entertainment. A few cafés were open but offered no food, only diluted coffee or tea. More importantly, they offered female company. The soldiers looked for company, and the women looked for supplies, cigarettes, or clothing. Anything that could be of use or could be traded for food.

I reached the corner of Ku'damm and Joachimstahlerstrasse, where Berlin's most famous cafés, the Kranzler and the Bristol, used to be. Unbelievably, they still existed, and under their business signs I saw a notice: "English and American military only." Seven years ago, when I left Berlin, the notice under the signs had said: "No Jews or dogs allowed."

I entered the Bristol. Only few tables were occupied; I chose one near the window. The café's furniture was exactly as before the war: dark wood tables and chairs; at the door, the coat hanger and the hat stand; on the wall, the wooden bars for the newspapers. A young, blonde woman handed me a cardboard menu and asked what I wanted to eat. The menu offered basic food, but the German cook managed to make it pleasant. The meal was abundant and inexpensive. I decided to establish my headquarters in this café during my stay in Berlin.

I took out my notebook to plan my days. I had come to Berlin to look for my Uncle Fritz. My unit companions had also asked me to deliver letters to addresses that might or might not exist, for relatives that might or might not have survived. I did not know if I would be able to fulfill all requests. In trying to get to Berlin and in the few hours I was in Berlin, I realized how difficult this would be.

An hour later I left the Bristol to head back to Uncle Fritz's house. As I walked, the feeling of triumph that had invaded me before, dissolved as I became deeply aware of the life circle that I was closing in that moment and place: Berlin–kibbutz–Al Alamein–Anzio–Rome–Berlin.

The evening darkness descended. The cafés on the Ku'damm became more animated as more American, English, and French soldiers flocked to the area looking for German Fräuleins. There was no room for German men, except as servers or pimps. I turned into a side street: it was empty and dark; there were no streetlights. Tiny rays of light sneaked through cracks in the boarded-up windows or through a few minuscule glass pieces, smaller than a hand-held flashlight.

I was only steps away from my uncle's apartment and was now overcome by anxiety. My body trembled in expectation of the reunion. How would this encounter be? How would my uncle look? I turned the corner; I could see his building with its arched gate and his apartment on the ground floor with a partially lit window. The light created a grotesque scene in this lugubrious and bombed city.

I crossed the building's threshold: on the right, my uncle's door. I rang the bell; the same old woman opened up to let me in. The door to my uncle's room was wide open; Uncle Fritz was sitting on a chair next to a table. As I walked towards him, he stood up, leaning firmly onto the table. We embraced in silence, we uttered not a sound. After long seconds, I said "Onkel," and he responded "Rudi." Tears in his eyes. Whether I cried or not, I do not remember. We let go of each other and I sat on a chair in front of him. We looked at each other for a long time, confirming that this was real and not a dream. The past seven years had changed us both as if it had been 20 years.

I was only a teenager when I left Germany; now, my military uniform multiplied the effect of the time that had passed. My uncle was a shadow of his old self. He had been a strong, robust, and erect man before, and now he was emaciated and stooped. His eyes transitioned from bright joy at this encounter to gray sadness as we took stock of all that had happened and all that had been lost. We were many and very united; now we were only two. My family was far away in South America, and his... much farther.

The lady who had let me in had not moved; she did not want to miss a detail of this reunion. Now she offered us a cup of tea. It was cold in the room, as there was no heating, so the hot infusion was very welcome. Three other survivors who shared the apartment approached us; they all wanted to join in my uncle's joy, and perhaps renew their own hopes for a similar miracle. The three figures were as transparent and diminished as my uncle.

Uncle Fritz dragged his prosthetic leg as he sat down. He had lost a leg as a cadet in the German Army in World War I. He had fought with unconditional enthusiasm for Germany, his homeland, and was awarded an Iron Cross. But his fighting, his Iron Cross, and his lost leg – none of that mattered to the Nazis who dragged him to the concentration camp in March of 1943.

Uncle Fritz had been a lead architect for the Central Bank in Berlin. The Nazis prohibited Jews from practicing their professions, and Uncle Fritz had been assigned to work in Berlin's war factories. In 1942, he and his wife were taken from their workplaces, placed on a truck, and taken to an Umschlagsplatz, a large square where prisoners were held before being sent to concentration camps. That was the last time he saw his wife, Berthe. Uncle Fritz was sent to Terezín, in Czechoslovakia, and Berthe to Auschwitz, in Poland.

Terezín was a unique camp set in an 18th-century fortress near Prague, where the Nazis imprisoned intellectuals from the European cultural elite and presented it as a "model camp" for propaganda purposes. Although it was not a death camp, over 33,000 inmates perished in Terezín from malnutrition, disease, or mistreatment. Amid miserable conditions and in constant fear of being deported "east" to the death camps, the prisoners held on to their spirit and created in Terezín a surreal world of intellectual debate and expression, on the thin edge between life and death. At the end of 1944, the Nazis began the liquidation of the camp, deporting 24,000 people to the death chambers in Auschwitz.

Terezín – and Uncle Fritz – was liberated by the Russian Army on May 8, 1945.

As soon as transportation was available, the Russian Army sent the Terezín survivors back to their places of origin. Most returned hoping to find a family member or a friend who might have survived. An army truck took Uncle Fritz to Berlin. In Berlin, Uncle Fritz approached the American authorities, who verified that his former apartment still existed and then ordered the German family who had taken it over to leave. The apartment was then reassigned to four survivors. Uncle Fritz was assigned two rooms – his former living and dining rooms – and other survivors were assigned the other rooms within the apartment. Housing was extremely scarce and there were strict regulations requiring people to share space. The building's superintendent showed up and cynically said to Uncle Fritz, "Mr. Haymann, how nice to see you back; we were worried about you." He had taken Uncle Fritz's furniture; now he brought part of it back.

It struck me that Uncle Fritz's windows had glass, despite this being such a scarce material. He explained that on his return to Berlin he went to visit his former workplace, where he met the engineers who had worked with him before the war. They were now directing reconstruction works throughout the city, and as a surprise gesture to him, they installed glass panes in his windows.

I stayed with Uncle Fritz for 12 days. I slept in the extra bed he had set up hoping that his wife would return. She never did. I shared breakfast with him every day and ate my other meals at the Bristol, so as not to take from his meager food rations. From Italy I had brought, with much difficulty, two large backpacks full of food and other items for him, but once in Berlin I realized that the scarcity would continue for a very long time. I tried to figure out how to continue helping my uncle from afar. As soldiers, we were forbidden to send packages to civilians, so I went to visit Rabbi Joseph Shubow, the chaplain in the US Army in Berlin and known for helping survivors. On hearing my story, he kindly offered to be the recipient of my packages via military mail and to deliver them to my uncle.

Rabbi Shubow was greatly surprised by my visit. I was the first soldier from the Jewish Brigade he had ever met. We talked at length about life and history. Ten years before, my schoolteacher had said to us, "Here you are students of history"; two years ago, my colonel in the Intelligence Service said, "Here you are witnesses of history." Rabbi Shubow now said to me, "You are makers of history."

For 12 days my uncle and I talked for hours. We retold our stories again and again, because we needed to voice them, understand, overcome, and record them deeply in our memory for the future.

Uncle Fritz's closest friend was an engineer named Falk Cichoki, who was not Jewish. Risking everything, Falk had supported my uncle during the three years he was in forced labor in a war factory, before his deportation to Terezín. When he learned of Fritz's deportation, Falk went to his house and in a quick and daring action, grabbed Fritz's leg prosthesis, hid in it three small pieces of jewelry, and took it to his own house. When Fritz returned to Berlin, Falk returned the prosthesis to him, and the three jewelry pieces: his grandfather's tie clip, a pin, and a thin gold necklace that my grandfather had given his wife when they married in 1881, which had been passed on to my mother when she married my father.

Uncle Fritz got up, searched in a drawer, and handed me the necklace: "One day, when you meet your parents again, please return this to its rightful owner." And I did. Three years later, in 1948, when I finally met my parents again, I handed the necklace to my mother. Years later, when I married, she gave the gold choker to my wife; and when my own son married, his wife received it. The golden necklace has graced four generations of women in our family.

Uncle Fritz and I went to visit Falk in Gatow, a quiet Berlin suburb. The British administration had named him mayor of Gatow for his impeccable credentials. I noticed that his family also lacked many essential items and later sent him several large packages from Italy through Rabbi Shubow. I felt fortunate to be able to return, at least in a small measure, his generous support to my uncle during the most difficult times.

I asked Uncle Fritz about our relatives and friends. Uncle Fridolin and his wife? "Deported to the death camps; none returned." Aunt Berthe's brother? "He and his family were deported to the death camps." Uncle James? "When they came for him, he was hanging from a beam." Asking and listening became a painful ritual.

While in Berlin, I also tried to locate my mother's Protestant family. What had happened to my uncle, my aunt, and my cousins from her side of the family? I initiated my search by looking for the place where my mother's brother Karl lived before the war. It was far away, there was no transportation, and I had to walk a long distance through piles and piles of war debris. The whole neighborhood was in ruins.

I found a huge heap of rubble where Karl's home used to be. Emerging from the rubble were stakes with boards with names and addresses written on them: "Family X, now in Z." I found a board with Karl's name on it, took note of the new address, walked back through the blocks of rubble, and searched for the new address. There I found again a mound of rubble and another stake and board with an address. The next day I searched for this new address and found a semi-destroyed building with Karl's family name on a door on the second floor.

I knocked on the door. A stooped man opened – my Uncle Karl. Surprised to see an English sergeant, he sullenly asked what I was looking for. I did not answer immediately, giving him time for a second look. He did not recognize me. I said, "Uncle Karl, I'm Rudi, your nephew." Silence, disbelief, amazement. He held on to door frame with both hands. Then, he released one hand and extended it, while he continued to hold on to the frame with the other, as the emotional impact washed over him. I hugged him. He did not say a word. From the inside of the room a tired voice asked: "Karl, who is it?" "It's Rudi, my sister's son." Karl's wife was sick and consumed by the war horrors. Her son had fought as a paratrooper for the Germans on the Russian front, her home had been bombed twice, and her two daughters, Rut and Ulla, had been raped by the Red Army soldiers who took over Berlin. She was devastated, saw no future ahead, and did not get out of bed anymore.

I asked Karl about his brother, Willie, and my cousin, Hans. I wanted to see them, but time was scarce. Karl agreed to contact them, and we set a date to meet again. On the agreed day, however, Willie did not show up. Months later, Willie wrote to me: "Rudi, Karl never informed me about your visit. He did not want you to learn from me that he was a Nazi party member."

My cousin Hans did show up. He was a successful black-market dealer and had recently married a Russian woman. Years later, when I visited Berlin again during the Cold War, he was living a tycoon's life. I believe he was a secret agent for the Soviets in West Germany, a belief confirmed when he contacted me with the manager of the Soviet newspaper *Izvestia*, when I visited Moscow in the 1970s, during Leonid Brezhnev's era in the Soviet Union.

I continued to explore Berlin. I visited Eyke von Rekowplatz in the Hansa district, where I had lived a happy childhood. All the buildings were bombed, but the square was intact, with its Litfassaule, the cylindrical advertising column plastered with notices, and the old water pump from the time when this was farmland. My family's former home on Agricolastrasse #16 had been bombed, as had the small cinema Die Kurbel, where I had spent much time as a kid.

What feelings did this trigger in me? It is difficult to recall accurately as I write now. I have recalled my experiences so many times over the years. Each time we look back, we have a different view of our own past. Memory, our delicate gift, registers the past, but is also colored by our present gaze. I know I felt some satisfaction, the pleasure of revenge. In 1938 the Nazi council had forced my parents to leave their apartment, as they did not want Jews living there. As I stood there in 1945, everything was in ruins, and nobody lived there.

It was now time for my departure from Berlin. Twelve days had seemed like a long time when I first arrived. But days, hours, are not a true measure of emotional time. The days felt like a short breath, a mere whiff of air. I consoled Uncle Fritz, telling him that I would return to see him again. We embraced, hoping for our next reunion.

But that visit turned out to be my first and last. The situation in Europe and in the British Army evolved and I did not return to Berlin. No other family members survived the war; Uncle Fritz lived on alone. My parents tried to bring him to Chile, but it was impossible to obtain a visa. My parents had no resources to travel to Berlin to visit him.

Uncle Fritz withered alone and died a few years later.

LETTERS AT THE END OF WAR

CHILE, 1945

Privacy is a magnificent luxury.
Letter from Hilla

On my return, I received the first letters from my family after the official end of the war.

Dear son: You cannot imagine the joy unleashed in my heart when I learned about your visit with Onkel Fritz. I know you made every effort to reach him and help him. The sad news about all our friends and acquaintances is unfortunately not unexpected. Does Onkel Fritz think he can live in Germany, after all that has happened there? We are too far to grasp the realities of being there.

And what about you, my son? How much longer is your Army service term? Will you return to your kibbutz? It may be possible to obtain a visa to Chile as an immigrant. It is very expensive, though. Some sons and daughters of other immigrants are starting to come. Much love from your Vati.

My mother added her own words.

My adored son: Can you believe it? Now that the war is over, your letter arrived in only two weeks! You finally had the opportunity to take time to recount for us in detail your war missions and experiences. Tough situations you had to live through, my boy. But the dear God has protected you, my "Sonntagskind," my fortunate son. Finally, this terrible war is over, and the Nazis will get the punishment they deserve.

How comforting it was to learn that you met with Onkel Fritz! I am jealous of all those who have the privilege to see you and embrace you before I do, but I happily give that privilege to him. February 2nd is his birthday, please do not forget to send him good wishes.

Dear Rudi, what did your homeland look like? it must be terrible in Germany now... But nothing attracts me now to a country of sadists and murderers. I am delighted that my brothers are alive, and I am sad for my nieces, raped by the Russian soldiers. But worse horrors were imposed on Jewish girls... So many innocent victims in this war. We are shocked and horrified with the news coming from Europe.

My father described for me the family properties in Ratibor, which he had been forced to sell to the Nazis. He hoped that something could be done about this loss. But the town ended up part of Poland after the war – now known in Polish as Racibórz – and Poland paid no war reparations to Jews.

Dear son: We were forced to sell our properties in Ratibor under a Municipal order overseen by City Counselor, Mr. Maywald. We owned Units #1 and #5 in the building located at the crossing of Troppauer and Blumenstrasse, as well as two plots across the street, and a plot on Troppauerstrasse #39. The buyers and the sales price were forced on us by the Nazi Government. We were paid only 89,000 marks and had to pay all taxes out of this total, against common practice. The deal was notarized by Mr. Pawlik and Mr. Schmidt. The properties' actual value was double the sale price. Of the total sale funds, I was allowed to cash only 6,000 marks – which I used to cover our emigration expenses – and the rest was frozen in a German account, which was later confiscated by the Nazis. We also know that the buyer mortgaged the

Five years after my parents and sister arrived in Chile, they were finally able to rent a small apartment, 52 square meters. After years of living crammed in one room in a boardinghouse, this little flat was a wonderful luxury. They were elated.

Dear Rudi: It is now six weeks since we moved into our new apartment on Quirihue #69. It is beautiful and exactly what I dreamt for all these years. It is a ten-minute walk from Vati's job at the Farmacia Central, which saves him time and money. We will set up a sleeping couch in the living room when you finally get here... I am frustrated that it will take yet another year before you can visit us. But, knowing that you are out of danger and safe in Europe will make it easier to wait. We are healthy and well. Love from your Mutti.

Dear Rudi, my brother: We feel great here. It is nice and cozy. We have very few pieces of furniture, but there is no space for more anyway. Mutti's curtains are now gracing our windows. Living in our own space, with our own kitchen and bathroom, feels wonderful. Privacy is a magnificent luxury.

My dearest son: I am overwhelmed by the many letters! You see, there is no greater joy for me than receiving letters from you. Dear son, at long last, this terrible war over. Take care of yourself and stay healthy for the new times to come. I yearn to reunite us all around a table and share our adventures and misadventures. This may still take a long time. For now, it is only a dream, but one day, it will be a reality. Regards from your Vati.

Meanwhile, I had returned to our headquarters in Rome. Colonel Roberts called me and said, "I have two items of news for you. You have been granted British-Palestinian citizenship for your war services. Your new passport just arrived. Congratulations." He gave me a minute to look at the document, which listed my data in three languages – English, Hebrew, and Arabic – and indicated my address as "Kibbutz Kfar Menachem" and my profession as "Soldier."

Colonel Roberts then said, "As for the second piece of news, you have a new assignment: Trieste."

TRIESTE

ITALY, 1945

You have been makers of history.
Rabbi Joseph Shubow, Berlin, 1945

The war had ended, and Europe was seeking to heal its wounds, both the physical and the psychological. Everybody wanted to rebuild their lives, their families, their homes, their villages, their work, and seek happiness and joy. Everywhere in England, Germany, France, and Italy. Everywhere, except in Trieste.

In Trieste the war continued. In Trieste the sound of machine guns still raged with fury, and wounds were opened rather than healed. Dreams turned into bombs, and the desire for peace turned into armed struggle. Located at the divide between Eastern and Western Europe, Trieste had been under Austro-Hungarian rule for centuries and then annexed by Italy after World War I, with a mixed population composed of Slavs, Slovenes, and Italians. Following the expulsion of the Nazis in 1943, Trieste was being torn in a three-way war: Austrians fought for the land they called Sudtirol; Italians fought for the same land they called Alto Adige; and Yugoslavs fought for the Istra Riveca peninsula, which the Italians called Gorizia.

During the day, commerce, industry, and agriculture functioned relatively well under the strong presence of the British Army. But at dusk, when civilians withdrew to their homes and the British soldiers returned to their barracks, the city became an open combat field for the various militias who fought for control of a street, a strategic building, or a neighborhood. They erected barricades and organized attacks and counterattacks. Each faction wanted to plant its own flag in this corner of Europe as a basis for their claims in the upcoming peace treaties and redefinition of national borders. The British soldiers were risking their lives for a cause that had nothing to do with their interests.

To this Trieste, I was destined to go.

Yes, the war was over. Seventy-five million people were dead. It is unimaginable. You can write the figure but not comprehend it. But the dead were dead and, cynically speaking, they were no longer a challenge. The real and immediate challenge was the 15 million war survivors who were not where they should be or wanted to be. These 15 million displaced people started to move. Endless columns of people marched for weeks and months across Europe, trying to get out of the place they had ended up at the war's end, and to reach a different destination – maybe the home they had been forced to leave, maybe their city of origin, or where their family might be. Millions of people walked 400, 800, or 1,500 kilometers in all directions across Europe. It took them four, eight, or twelve months to reach their destination, if they succeeded. Forced laborers and ex-prisoners marched from Holland to Yugoslavia, or from Hungary to Italy; former German soldiers and Nazi collaborators marched from Greece to Austria, or from Albania to Germany. It was a mass migration on a scale never seen before. There was no transportation in Europe yet: most roads and train tracks had been destroyed during the war, trucks had no tires, buses were non-existent, and gasoline was an expensive luxury sold only on the black market. The only way to get anywhere was to walk, and the masses walked.

Little by little, the railway lines were reconstructed and some trains began to run. The news spread like wildfire in all directions, and huge masses now marched towards these few train routes. The throngs of migrants flooded every thoroughfare and every route. And one of the main migration routes passed precisely through Trieste.

Our team of 12 Intelligence Service officers had been entrusted to a new unit, the Allied Refugee Screening Commission (ARSC), whose mission was to filter the avalanche of people arriving in Trieste from the Balkans and heading west to Italy, Austria, and Germany. Most displaced people wanted to reach Central Europe to restart their lives, but the occupation governments in Germany and Austria did not want to receive people of uncertain or certain Nazi past.

A huge refugee camp had formed in Trieste, and it was our responsibility to screen the migrants. Anybody migrating from north to south had a free pass to move on; anyone traveling from south to north, however, had to pass through a filter and get our stamp of approval to continue across borders.

Eight of us worked on field recognition tasks: a Czech, a Pole, a Lithuanian, a French, two Maltese, and two Palestinian Jews. We were a melting pot within the British Army. Our mission was to uncover those who had been Nazi collaborators in the Balkans or SS members with stolen or falsified identification, disguised as refugee migrants passing through Trieste. It was a very difficult task. Over 1,000 people arrived every day, and we discovered only the crudest impostors. The rest fell through the cracks due to lack of time, staff, or means. It was interesting but frustrating and exhausting work.

One day I came across a convoy of army ambulances carrying soldiers who had been wounded in Trieste's night-time skirmishes. The drivers were Jewish Palestinian female soldiers. What a joy! It had been a long time since I had encountered one of my people. We talked for a while. They asked what I was doing, and then indicated that a friend was going to visit me. A week later a corporal showed up. He greeted me, disregarding any military formality. "I am Moshe from Kibbutz Tel Josef, vice-commander of Aliyah Bet," he said. Aliyah Bet was the code name for Jewish Holocaust survivors immigrating illegally to British Palestine during that time. "How many Jews in your unit?" he asked. "Two," I replied. "One of you will work exclusively for our cause," he said.

I immediately understood where my place was and where my priorities and loyalties were. The military confrontations had come to an end. Now, leaders and soldiers were engaged in the political struggle to position their own cause, preparing for the division of the spoils of war. "We are boarding Holocaust survivors on ships in Rimini," explained Moshe. "We have set up a shelter in Mestre for those who want to take this risk and wait their turn. Your role will be to identify Jewish survivor refugees in Trieste, explain to them that there is a route, and help them get to Mestre. Our companion Aviva will keep in touch with you. Shalom." And he left. This was a military order that I would fulfill.

I discussed the matter with my partner, and we agreed that he would continue to hunt down war criminals while I would follow Moshe's directions. The next day, I entered the huge refugee camp with my Jewish Brigade badge, with its blue-white-blue stripes and golden *Magen David* [Star of David]. There was no doubt who I was; Jewish survivors within the camp approached me, addressing me in Yiddish, the old language of European Jews: "*Di bist a Yid? Ij bin oijj a Yid*" [Are you Jewish? I am also a Jew.]

The elderly said, "I want to return to my hometown; maybe some family member survived." I gave them a pass to Munich, Frankfurt, or other cities in Central Europe, along with some useful advice. But the younger refugees all wanted to leave Europe and seek new horizons. For them, Europe offered no hope; they had few or no good memories from before the war and carried deep wounds in their souls. Some said, "Help me go to America." "I can give you a pass to cross Austria and Germany, but I cannot give you a visa," I replied. "You will have to walk 600 kilometers to the American sector."

But most young people said, "I want to go to Israel." I gave them a pass to Italy and instructed them to walk 100 kilometers to the camp in Mestre and wait there until the Aliyah Bet leaders assigned them to one of the boats commanded by brave Italian captains who dared to cross the sea in fragile and overloaded vessels, to British

Palestine. To the most weakened, I said, "Wait for me tomorrow, two kilometers north of the city, past the military control," and I picked them up in my official truck and drove them 50 kilometers towards Mestre. Sometimes I would meet Aviva in the ambulance convoy. These daring female soldiers carried weakened refugees hidden among their sick. A wink or a compliment at the checkpoint avoided further inspection of their ambulance. Even the cold English checkpoint soldiers succumbed to their feminine charms.

La ultima lettera [the last letter]

Beautiful Claudia:

Four months ago, I embraced you for the last time, as I departed on my next mission. I have since traveled across four countries, with each mission riskier than the prior one. Three weeks ago, the Army informed me that I would not be sent back to Italy at all. I have been assigned to return to the Middle East.

I wrote you a sad farewell letter, my dear Claudia, and yesterday, on my way from Egypt to Lebanon, I received your response letter containing only five words: "Rudi, che ti ho fatto?" *[What did I do to you?] I will answer you, Claudia.*

When we entered Rome victoriously 20 months ago, I found you. I learned that meeting you was the greatest victory of my war, and that Rome is the most beautiful city in the world, "la cittá piu bella", *because you walk on its ancient streets. I learned that light blue and black is the perfect color pairing, because they are the colors of your eyes and your hair. I learned that your embrace is the way to the greatest happiness.* Tutto quello mi hai fatto tu, bellisima *Claudia. That much did you do to me, beautiful Claudia.*

A Dio. *Goodbye, Rudi*

THE LAST MISSION
SUEZ–BEIRUT, 1946

Do not be wise in words,
be wise in deeds.
Jewish proverb

During the war we did not talk much about life after the war. How could we, when we did not know if we would survive? The war was all consuming, immediate, and urgent, and talking about the future was too speculative, too fragile a topic. But now, at last, peace had arrived, and with it the big question: What will become of me?

The British Army gave clear directives: "There will be no immediate massive demobilizations." A scoring system ranked all soldiers based on years of service, family responsibilities, and other factors to determine each soldier's date of demobilization. My score was low, very low, because three and a half years of service was few in a war that lasted almost six. I did not score much on other factors either, as I was very young and single. I was scheduled to serve for another year and a half.

Along with this notice, I was also granted a month-long vacation. A month! I was thrilled. I prepared my backpack and left Italy for my kibbutz in British Palestine.

Over three years had passed since I had left. Much had changed on the kibbutz and in British Palestine. The country was experiencing great economic activity; new roads and new housing were being built, tractors were working the fields, and much more. It was wonderful to meet my kibbutz companions again. I was welcomed warmly, and everybody wanted to know when I would return. I was still unsure about what I would do in the future, so I left the question floating in the air.

My vacation passed quickly. I reported to the local British Army base to return to my service in Italy. I was informed that the next ship to Italy would depart in a month, and that I would serve locally in the meantime. I mentioned to the local commandant that I could help on intelligence related tasks. He did not like this idea; relations between the British government and the Jewish community were deteriorating rapidly. A political cauldron was simmering; the Jewish community demanded recognition for their contributions in the war. The Arab community was silent, as they had rather been enemy sympathizers. But in politics, the adversary must be treated with more care than the sympathizer, and there were one million Arabs versus 700,000 Jews in British Palestine. The Jewish community had asked the British government to eliminate the immigration quotas for Holocaust survivors who had nowhere in the world to go. The Arabs tried to prevent this. The situation was complex. Each group fought on two political fronts: Arabs against British and Jews; Jews against Arabs and British; and the British tried to stay afloat.

In this scenario, the British Army did not want any Jews in their intelligence units stationed in the region. So instead of doing intelligence work, I was sent to Suez, in Egypt. In Suez there were large camps holding German and Italian prisoners from the Africa campaign, as well as prisoners from Eastern Europe and the Balkans who were Nazi sympathizers. The British Army was now dismantling these camps and repatriating the prisoners to their home countries. Only fascist leaders would be retained as prisoners to prevent their political influence in their home countries. I was assigned to repatriate a couple of Yugoslav soldiers. My mission was to take them from Suez to Turkey and hand them over to another

British unit, which would take them to Yugoslavia. I thought this was a great task that offered the opportunity to visit Lebanon and part of Turkey. I had heard fascinating stories about these exotic places.

I was given a jeep and a driver. A young and surly lieutenant handed me the two Yugoslav prisoners without handcuffs. He gave no warning on their political or military record. Looking back, I wonder if it was negligence or underlying sympathy for the prisoners, who turned out to be fervent anticommunists, who would probably be sentenced to life in prison by Tito, the new communist leader of Yugoslavia. As an experienced soldier, I should have inquired about their history, but I did not. Maybe I wanted to avoid further conversation with that unpleasant lieutenant, or maybe we all hurried because the transfer was made under blazing sun and in a temperature of 50 degrees. The fact is that I did not realize the kind of men I was taking charge of.

We left in our jeep. The driver and I sat in the front and the two Yugoslavs sat in the back. We spent the first night at a military post in the Sinai desert, the second night near Gaza, and the third close to the Lebanese border. We crossed into Lebanon, which was under French rule at the time. My plan was to reach a police post just south of Beirut early the next morning to hand over the Yugoslavs, and then spend the rest of the day visiting Beirut, "the Paris of the Middle East," famous for its vibrant culture.

The Lebanese countryside was peaceful; the fields were plowed and well planted. The Lebanese farmers owned their land and were not subjects of exploitive Arab *effendi* landowners as in Palestine. We saw no policemen or soldiers anywhere. There was little traffic, and we advanced rapidly. Our jeep climbed up a hill and slowed down to take a curve. And then, disaster struck. The Yugoslavs jumped on us, my driver lost control of the vehicle and it veered off into a ditch. The crash threw us all out of our seats and up in the air. I lost consciousness; a black cloud engulfed me. I have no memory of anything beyond that.

The Yugoslav prisoners knew they would be imprisoned in Yugoslavia and figured they had nothing to lose in risking an escape. They noticed the lack of police in Lebanon and decided that this was their opportunity.

I do not know how long I was unconscious. Then, I heard voices around me, soothing me and instructing me not to move. I was put on a stretcher and carried to an ambulance. White walls, hospital smell, hushed voices. My skin against a flat, cold table. And then, an icy shock as my entire body was put in a plaster cast from my armpits to my hips. The cast would be my new uniform for the next 70 days.

I had a serious spinal injury. But I had also been very lucky; I could have been paralyzed, but the doctor assured me that I would walk again. The Yugoslav prisoners were also seriously injured and were now in custody. My driver, however, perished in the accident. The military investigation reported on the serious military and political consequences if the Yugoslavs had escaped. Thankfully, they did not.

I had been in the army for three and a half years and had been lucky to survive the war alive and well. And now that peace had arrived, this happened, impacting my life and my health forever. After 70 days in the cast, followed by 30 days in intense therapy, I was discharged. "Dismissed; unfit for the army." Everything had changed completely for me.

Everything had changed also for all Jewish soldiers. Thousands of Jewish soldiers were demobilized from the British Army, regardless of their score. The Colonial Office in British Palestine wanted to contain the immigration of Holocaust survivors coming from shattered Europe. This immigration was supported in great measure by open and covert help of the Jewish Brigade soldiers stationed across all of Europe, from Italy to the Netherlands. To prevent this, the British leaders decided to demobilize all the Palestinian Jewish soldiers. Shiploads of experienced and hardened veterans were now returning to British Palestine.

We were summoned for the last time. The sign above the barrack door read: "Discharge Center." Four years ago, it read "Recruiting Center." This was where I was welcomed, and this was where I was being let go. We wore our best and cleanest uniform and were called in one by one. A young officer who clearly had never been to the war front was sitting behind a desk. He got up, gave me the military salute, reached his hand out to me with a forced smile, and said, "On behalf of His Majesty, I thank for your services." Then, he cut off a corner of my military passport to invalidate it, and returned it to me, along with the balance of my savings account, one month's salary for severance, and a certificate of good performance. He then pointed to the exit door on the right. It all took only three and a half minutes: not even one minute per year of service.

In the adjacent room, I was given a civilian suit made of thick navy-blue wool, which would be totally useless in the hot Mediterranean climate; a white shirt, a tie, a pair of thick-soled shoes, and a wide-brimmed hat. I was allowed to keep my underwear, my badges, and my medals. I looked at myself in a mirror. Unbelievable. I had not worn civilian clothes in four years. I looked again, to confirm and absorb my new image.

On August 7, 1946, I wrote the last words in my war diary: "*E finita la comedia*" [The play is over].

To my war diary

For almost four years you have been my faithful companion, my little diary; but today is the last day.

The upper left pocket of our combat suit was designated for our military passport. The right pocket, however, was for our personal use. That's where I carried you, my diary, from Palestine to Suez, across Tunis and Libya, across the Mediterranean, all along Italy, and then to Greece, Austria, Berlin, and finally back to Palestine.

Sitting in the army cafeteria sipping tea with lemon, I take a last look at you, my faithful friend for years. In your small pages I wrote down dates, names, and notes that would aid my memory in future times. I observe the different ink colors – blue, green, and black, depending on the pen available. I wrote in four languages: In English, the language of the British Army, I wrote data and work chronicles. In Hebrew, the language of my kibbutz, I commented on personal issues. In German, the language of my childhood, I wrote names and expressions, part of my intense intelligence labor. And in the beautiful Italian language I wrote about love.

This is the longest entry, the farewell. Am I sad or joyful at this moment? Neither. Not sad; four years were enough to complete this life experience. Not joyful either; much uncertainty awaits me out there in my new life. What do I really feel? Contentment. Yes, that's it. Contentment for walking out upright. Content and grateful for life. Goodbye my war diary, my companion and friend.

Pal / 38691 Sgt. Rudi Haymann
CSDIC Intelligence Corp.
Central Mediterranean Forces,
Royal British Army
1946

2

SOLDIER'S NAME and DESCRIPTION on ATTESTATION.

Army Number PAL/38691

Surname (in capitals) ...... HAYMANN

Christian Names (in full) ...... RUDOLF

Date of Birth 21. 8. 1921

Place of Birth.
Parish ...... Beit-Zaira
In or near the town of ...... TIBERIAS
In the county of ...... PALESTINE

Trade on Enlistment ...... FARMER

Nationality of Father at birth ......

Nationality of Mother at birth ......

Religious Denomination ...... JEW

Approved Society ......

Membership No. ......

Enlisted at ...... SARAFAND On 6. 4. 43

For the :—
* Regular Army.   * Supplementary Reserve.
* Territorial Army.   * Army Reserve Section D.
            * Strike out those inapplicable.

For ...... years with the Colours and ...... years in the Reserve.

Signature of Soldier ...... Rudolf Haymann

Date 7. 4. 43

Page from my Soldier's Service Book with my number PAL 38691 and a
false place of birth, in case I was taken prisoner by the Nazis.

RETURN TO CIVILIAN LIFE
BRITISH PALESTINE, 1947

Once a soldier, always a soldier.
English proverb

The war was over, but strong political storms were blowing in British Palestine. The political context transformed us from soldiers into civilians, but also into adversaries of our former army. New priorities and new loyalties emerged.

"E finita la comedia" [The play is over] were the last words I wrote in my diary as I was dismissed from the army. However, this was only the end of one chapter in the grand human play. Now the difficult postwar chapter began. I was no longer a soldier of the British Army; I became again an active militant of the Haganah, the Jewish defense forces.

Returning to civilian life after four years as a soldier is shocking. I remember that time vividly. My comrades and I looked at each other again and again, dressed in our new civilian clothes. We had met in the army and had never seen each other like this before. We looked different, and in fact, we were different now. And if looking at my comrades was cause for astonishment, looking at myself in the mirror was even more shocking and revealing. I was no longer the idealistic youngster who had joined the army four years before. A war-seasoned and experienced man was now staring back at me from the mirror. So much had happened, so much I had witnessed, so much I had lived. A mature man was starting a new life that day.

It was noon. Our group hesitantly advanced from our military base to the intercity bus stop. Bobby, my soulmate, was going to his parents' house in Tel Aviv to ponder about his future. Dov, my other friend, opted to go to Haifa to commence his new life. Eric had a girlfriend to share a room with. Of our four-leaf clover of tight friends, I was the only one who had nowhere to go. I could return to the kibbutz, but after my war experience I no longer envisioned my future as a farmer. Where, then? The buses came, and one by one my companions boarded and headed off to their new lives. After a while, only two of us without a destination remained at the bus stop.

I did not know the other man, but I decided to pair up with him. We boarded a bus to Tel Aviv, and we looked for an inexpensive hotel room to share. We found a clean room with a shared bathroom. Perfect; we were used to shared quarters after years of military life. I left my bag in the room and went out to plan my immediate future. My first challenge was to find a place to live. It was practically impossible to find housing in Tel Aviv due to extreme shortages. But if you do not have a place to sleep, to wash yourself and change your clothes, you cannot look for work. I could not afford to stay in the hotel for long. I had to find another solution.

I could sleep on the beach. There were miles of beaches with clean, white sand along the Tel Aviv coastline. I tried this out one night, but it was impossible to sleep well in the sand. Then I considered sleeping in the back seat of a bus and went to a nearby bus station to check. Everyone was willing to help demobilized soldiers. "Yes, you can sleep on the bus, as long as you are out by five o'clock in the morning, when the cleaning crew comes in." It was not great, but it was better than the beach. I spent several nights on the bus.

I met an ex-comrade from the Jewish Brigade and we

exchanged views on our reintegration into civilian life. "I am working as a guard at a school; I get a small salary and a room to sleep in," he said. "The students are on vacation for the next two weeks. You can sleep in a classroom and use the school bathrooms." I accepted gratefully. What a welcome respite!

A few days later I ran into an ex-soldier standing in line in front of an apartment building. "Someone died here last night; his room will be vacated, and I am applying for the room," he said. It seems grotesque today, but this did happen at that time. The regulations at the time required every apartment to house as many people as rooms in the unit. This was strictly enforced, as the need for housing was enormous.

I learned that the Baruch family, who had been our friends in Berlin, was now living in Tel Aviv. I had not seen them for nine years and went to visit them. Mr. Baruch was a renowned doctor, with an office on Allenby Avenue, the most important street in the city. His family lived in an apartment above the office. Mrs. Baruch was very excited to see me after so many years and welcomed me warmly with coffee. They had left Germany in 1937 and settled in Tel Aviv; little by little the doctor had built a solid reputation and was able to buy the office and apartment. Their son, my former school friend, was studying and working, and their youngest daughter was about to get married. "And you, Rudi," Mrs. Baruch gently asked, "are you going back to the kibbutz?" "No," I said, "I want to work in the city, but I have been unable to find a place to live." She pondered and said, "I may have a solution. My daughter is getting married, her room will be available, and per law, we will have to house someone else. I would rather have you than someone we do not know. Let me talk to my husband; give me a couple days."

Two days later we talked again. "You can be our tenant," she said, "if you accept our conditions. Instead of occupying my daughter's room, which we need as a home office, you will sleep in a sofa-bed in the doctor's office; you will have a closet for your belongings; I will give you breakfast every day, and we will not charge you any rent, honoring our long friendship." I wanted to jump up and hug her, but I was frozen and teared up. She handed me her handkerchief.

There were organizations at that time that assisted discharged soldiers in finding work. I sought their help and filled out an application, listing my qualifications. How could I qualify for a design job, if I knew only how to milk cows and fight a war? I included my drawing and design studies in Rome, and apparently this was good enough. I was directed to the British Cartography Department: "They need people who know how to draw."

At the Cartography Department I had to report on my military background and take a drawing test. I was then offered a job as draftsman at the lowest rank, with a miserable salary. I asked for a few hours to decide. I went back to the employment office and explained to the man in charge that I wanted and needed to work, but the minimal salary made me hesitate. "Wait a moment," he said, and returned with another man. "I am Joshua, from the intelligence unit of the Haganah. Take the job, we need you there, to obtain valuable maps and information. Regarding the salary, we will find a solution." They guided me to file a request to the British Army for a scholarship for studies to change profession after having been dismissed due to my accident. It turned out to be great advice; the army would give me a six-month scholarship if I could prove that a registered institute or professional was training me.

My friend Bobby introduced me to Lotte Cohn, a prestigious architect in Tel Aviv. She interviewed me and said, "You do not know enough yet to work with my team, but I will teach you. The scholarship money that the army would pay me to teach you, I will give back to you for your expenses. I do not need the money and I want to help our young soldiers in their reinsertion into civilian life." She was wonderful and generous.

Everything was falling into place for me. I worked every morning at the Cartography Department and every afternoon in the architecture studio. I earned two half-salaries that were sufficient to live on, and I did not have to pay rent to the Baruchs.

A wealth of new experiences opened for me. Mrs. Baruch became a warm and caring second mother to me. She prepared breakfast for me and a small snack to take to work. Lotte Cohn devoted much time to training me in design, and I learned much under her guidance. She had immigrated from Berlin in 1921 and was the first female architect in the country. She was a pioneer, leading an avant-garde design practice inspired by the Bauhaus and the *Binyan Haaretz* [Build the country] ideals to build a modern Jewish homeland. During the time I trained with her, she designed workers' settlements, the new Tel Aviv bus station, and the Dizengoff Plaza. Her team included four collaborators, another trainee, and me. I enjoyed the work enormously.

I then decided to aim at higher professional goals and train for the London Matric, the admissions test for British universities. I studied doggedly every night to complete my high school education to qualify for the exam. These activities were extremely intense and absorbing, but also very rewarding.

The work at the Cartography Department was more challenging. The department was responsible for preparing geographic and topographic survey maps and maintaining cadastral plans. This was very exacting, regulated, and slow work, and entirely different from the lively and creative architecture design environment at Lotte Cohn's office that I loved so much.

At the Cartography Department we worked in a huge room equipped with 40 large drafting tables. The department heads were all British; mid-level supervisors and staff were Arabs; there were only a handful Jews, all former soldiers like me, and only two women. We worked six days a week with one free day according to one's religion: Friday for Muslims, Saturday for Jews, and Sunday for Christians. Work was strictly guided by tradition and hierarchy, with five draftsmen ranks; the lowest one, which I was part of, drew in pencil, with pantograph; the fourth level drew topographic contour lines and building footprints with Chinese ink; the third level drew numbers; the second level drew labels and flourished titles and borders. The highest rank was the supervisor's assistants, who did not draw but checked quality, precision, and progress.

Talking was strictly forbidden. Tasks were distributed by the assistants, based on the supervisor's instructions. The supervisor was a plump, good-natured Arab man in his fifties, who sat on a raised platform in the center of the huge room, in his blue suit and a white shirt, which he changed every three hours. Never, during the year I worked there, did he get off his platform to approach any of the draftsmen. A superior was not supposed to talk directly to a low-ranked employee. His assistants went around to attend consultations, approve, or comment on the work, and enforce absolute silence. Any verbal exchange, even in the lowest voice, was reprimanded and garnered a negative annotation in one's service sheet.

The assistants were also responsible for scheduling rest time for the employees, following the Turkish-Ottoman institutional tradition of working calmly. Modern western pace and "productivity" were considered detestable and threatened the millenary traditions. Supporting the calm working style were the breakrooms. Nearly a third of the work time was spent in the breakrooms: not everybody at the same time, of course, but in carefully scheduled breaks, organized by the assistants.

There were two spacious bathrooms, each with an anteroom with benches and chairs, which functioned as the breakrooms. The premier breakroom included Turkish coffee service and was reserved for senior employees. The second breakroom was for junior staff and did not include coffee service. These golden rules were deeply rooted in the Turkish-Ottoman traditions practiced for over 400 years. Traditions were being challenged by the British rulers and the Jewish settlers, but here at the Cartography Department they were still thoroughly protected.

At first, this was an entertaining curiosity for me, but soon it became a nightmare to waste my precious hours in the breakroom, and worse, without coffee. But I decided to follow the rules so as not attract any attention while I strategized on how to obtain copies of the survey plans. I followed the classic practice of the "dead mole": do not make any move until you assess the context and define a good tactic. As soon as my provisional contract was upgraded to permanent, I began to act. It was clear that I would not have access to any documents beyond those on my drafting table, but I also realized that the plans I worked on were a rich source of information. My lowly job consisted in drawing annotations on the plans based on notes provided by field surveyors. As there was nothing artistic in my task, the assistants rarely visited my desk, except to pick up my finished work and give me the next assignment.

I developed a very productive technique. The sandwiches that Mrs. Baruch gave me each day were wrapped in waxed paper as was usual at that time. I carefully extended the waxed paper under the plan I was working on and then, as I drew, I pressed hard on my pen to mark on the underlying wax paper everything I drew. At the end of the day, I carefully folded and stored my wax paper in my bag, for all to see that I was a somewhat miserly man who recycled his lunch packaging. As soon as I got home, I retraced the marked lines and annotated numbers and names still fresh in my memory. Once a week I handed my work to my Haganah superior.

But everything changed abruptly in November 1947. My civilian life lasted barely 15 months.

The Cartography Department commissioned me to get some surveys from the Jerusalem office. I planned my trip for the upcoming Thursday, to stay in Jerusalem over the weekend with my girlfriend Margalit. It seemed like a good plan.

That Friday, November 29, 1947, the United Nations voted to end the British Mandate in Palestine and approved the partition of the territory into two independent states, one Jewish State and one Arab State. Although our Jewish community would have preferred a larger territory, we immediately accepted and abided by the United Nations resolution. The Arab community, however, rejected it in its entirety. On Saturday, we were celebrating in the streets at the realization of a centuries-old dream; but by Sunday, the furious Arab community erupted with shootings, armed attacks, and blockades.

The situation was critical. The Haganah immediately took control of all intercity transportation and set travel priorities based on security criteria. I was in Jerusalem and tried to get back to Tel Aviv. At the bus station I ran into Maxi, my old warmate and former commander of my platoon. What a joy to see him again! We stood together in the long line at the bus station, talking about the past and the future. At last, it was our turn: "Two tickets to Tel Aviv, please," we said. "I am sorry," said the clerk, "Maxi has priority and will travel tomorrow; Rudi will have wait two days." Maxi and I parted ways with a warm hug.

The next day a convoy of buses was ambushed and machine-gunned by Arab attackers. A horrible massacre, the first victims; the War of Independence had started.

Among the victims, Maxi.

TO AMERICA
ISRAEL TO ARGENTINA, 1948

How can I even try to express in a letter all that I feel for you?
My father's letter, 1946

Another war was starting. But I needed to see my family. I had left my parents in Berlin ten years earlier. For ten years we had communicated only through letters. For ten years I had not looked into my parents' eyes. I missed them and worried about them. Their letters reflected their nostalgia for their faraway son:

You can't imagine the joy we felt receiving your photograph! I would have given everything for this picture. I look at your image and it reminds me of my father, you look like him. The photograph also speaks to me about all what we have missed in the past ten years; I grieve for not seeing you grow to become the fine man you now are. I grieve for all our missed conversations about life, which you liked so much. I am jealous of all those who enjoy the privilege of seeing you. We miss you so badly; we need to talk and see you face to face.

My parents had initiated an application to obtain a visa for me to travel to Chile. The process turned out to be extremely complicated and took 16 months of paperwork, rejections, help from influential people, and more paperwork. Eventually, the visa was approved and sent to the Chilean consulate in Cairo, but the Consul in Cairo created more obstacles and my hard-won visa expired. My desperate parents managed to obtain an extension, and this time the coveted visa was sent to Milan, to be stamped on my British passport.

Dear son: Dealing with bureaucrats is extremely slow and frustrating; getting an immigration visa seems quite impossible. The war is finally over but seeing my son still seems an impossible dream. But we will not waver, no matter what new rules and requirements they discover every time we advance a step. There will be elections here in a month, so no public official will issue any approval now.

Dear brother: All our conversations revolve around the challenges of obtaining your visa. We have left no stone unturned; meetings at the British Embassy, Ministry of Interior, Ministry of International Relations... to no avail. They refused to approve a visa. I had to communicate this bad news to our parents, and they were devastated. The Portuguese Ambassador in Chile, who is Vati's client at the pharmacy, noticed him sad and depressed. When questioned, Vati explained the situation, and the Ambassador, indignant, intervened on our behalf and untangled the situation. We have your Visa! We are jubilant.

Dear son: Finally! Your visa was sent to Milan; it should be stamped on your passport in January. They may request your travel ticket to do so. Please label your luggage and ensure it is certified by the Consul. Otherwise, you will have difficulties getting it through customs here on arrival. It is best if you go to Genoa. As a single person you may find a space on a ship. Let me know when your visa is stamped in your passport. Otherwise, I will have to request an extension. My thoughts are focused on getting you to Chile. Once you are here, I will then concentrate on finding some way to bring Onkel Fritz as well.

It was very challenging to get transportation to Italy. After much effort, in December 1947, I was able to secure a place on a ship from Alexandria, Egypt, to Genoa, Italy, and from there I traveled to

Milan by land. My visa was finally stamped in my passport by a friendly Italian consul in early January 1948.

Now I needed to find space on a ship to South America. This was extremely difficult in those postwar days. There was no regular maritime service yet, no way to make a reservation, and available spaces were very scarce. Millions of people were trying to leave Europe, and waiting lists swelled with requests from people who had lost everything and wanted a new future; survivors of extermination camps who could not face the idea of life in Europe; war criminals with false documents; and adventurers of all kinds. Everyone wanted to leave, to wherever the wind was blowing.

"There are no ships to Chile," I was told. "Are there any ships to Buenos Aires, Argentina?" I asked. "Yes, but there is a waiting list." "How long?" "Twelve to fourteen months." I was desperate. After so many years of war, and so many tribulations trying to get a visa, it seemed I would never be able to see my family. I turned to the American Jewish Joint Committee, a wonderful organization that worked with the Red Cross and the United Nations to assist in transporting and resettling war refugees. Another miracle: they helped me obtain a space to Buenos Aires, Argentina, in a cargo vessel that had served to transport supplies to US troops during the war. It had now been repurposed to carry human cargo on its way to South America, and grain cargo on its way back, to feed a hungry Europe.

I finally departed in early February 1948. I stood on the deck looking out at the land I was leaving. On the pier below, people were hugging and wishing each other good luck. Most travelers were young men venturing to test their luck in the new world, hoping that they would later call for their wives and children. The elderly who had no strength to start a new life, stayed behind.

Nearly 800 passengers were on board, occupying every inch, in four huge cargo compartments for 200 people each, fitted with rows of three-tier bunk beds, plus a giant table made of wooden planks on trestles in the center. One of the four compartments was for women only, and the other three for men. There were no windows; bathrooms were minimal and insufficient. The upper deck was the only open space to renew the air in our lungs. Travel conditions were tight and tough, and the voyage was long, but nobody complained. Everyone felt privileged to be on this ship and to leave behind pain and immense losses. We carried nothing except hope for a new life. Everybody looked forward, full of expectations.

People formed groups according to their affinities. Most of the passengers were Italian; the rest were Poles, Jews, and people from the Balkans. I settled in with the other Jews, who were all Holocaust survivors. Although the different groups did not mix much, all co-existed peacefully during the month of travel. No one asked too many questions; everyone's personal story was accepted as true.

Of the 800 passengers, about 760 were headed to Argentina and about 40 to Brazil. I was the only one traveling farther to Chile. Some had relatives or friends willing to lend them a hand during the early days upon their arrival. Others carried papers with names of people to contact for help in the beginning. A few were studying Spanish. "With our Italian we will manage," said the Italians.

Ten minutes after departure, the ship stopped in the middle of the sea. A patrol boat arrived, and policemen climbed onto the ship to search for stowaways who may have circumvented the boarding controls. Those discovered were thrown into the sea; they had no choice but to swim to the patrol boat and ask for mercy to save their lives. From the deck we watched this show; we sympathized with the young adventurers and shouted words of consolation. Later, we discovered a couple stowaways that had managed to dodge the police search; everybody helped them throughout the rest of the trip, providing them with blankets and food.

Our first stop was in the Canary Islands, where we were allowed to disembark. Local youngsters approached us asking for help to get onto the ship. "Where are your belongings?" I asked one young man. "I have no belongings, to avoid any suspicions," he said. "When you return to the boat, hide me in the crowd; lend me your shirt, shoes, and pants, to blend in." But we could not help them;

we had to show our boarding passes; the guards easily discovered the men without a pass and beat them up. And our ship moved on.

Since I spoke Italian, I acted as interpreter for the passengers in my compartment. The Italian officer inquired how I had learned Italian, and when I told him I had been in Italy during the war, he invited me up to the command bridge and introduced me to the captain. We chatted and shared life stories; When I told him about my experience in Trieste, he said, "I was the captain of one of those boats carrying refugees across the Mediterranean, circumventing the British controls." The friendship with the captain helped me escape the unbearable intensity and bustle of the only deck. I went up to the command bridge every day for an hour and immensely enjoyed the tranquility and the conversation. Life circumstances rapidly change our priorities and what we value most.

As we traveled south, the days became warmer; it was February, high summer in the southern hemisphere. From the ship's deck I could glimpse the coast on the horizon, and I pondered the challenges and successes that awaited us beyond that distant line.

We arrived at the port of Rio de Janeiro, Brazil, at the crack of dawn. From the deck I scrutinized the profile of this famous city, hailed as the most beautiful in South America. The port was full of cranes, trucks, and rail cars, but there was no activity. Nobody was working. There was loud music, and people were walking around relaxedly in shorts, short sleeves, or shirtless. It was the beginning of Carnival, the yearly three-day Brazilian party. By afternoon, the port was totally empty; not even the port guards were there; everybody had left to join the Carnival. Some daring passengers descended from our ship onto the dock. Absolutely nobody stopped them. Others followed, and soon there was no one left on the ship. We stepped on American soil for the first time. I thought of the few stowaways that had traveled with us; they were surely already on the mainland, participating in the debauchery and the great reception this continent offered to the fearless and the adventurous. I smiled.

I walked towards a nearby beach. A huge party was in full swing – music, dancing, and more eroticism than I had ever seen in my life, practiced openly and publicly. My astonishment was mixed with doubt. How would I ever fit into a life like this? This was not what I envisioned for myself.

By dawn, everybody was back on the ship and our voyage continued to the port of Santos, Brazil, where we anchored for 40 hours but were not allowed to disembark. Members of the local Jewish community came on board to welcome the Jewish refugees. Upon learning that I was born in Berlin, like her, one woman invited me to spend the day with her family. "I am sorry, we are not allowed to descend," I said. "Oh, that's not an obstacle," she said. Half hour later I traveled with her to her home in Sao Paulo. I pondered whether this was life in South America.

Hours later, I was back on the ship, and we continued to our destination, Buenos Aires, Argentina. There, everyone disembarked.

Everyone, except for me.

REUNION

CHILE, 1948

Here I come to my own again.
Fed, forgiven and known again,
claimed by bone of my bone.
Rudyard Kipling, *The Prodigal Son*

"Sir, how do you intend to continue traveling to Chile?" asked the Argentinian immigration officer as he looked at my documents. "I have been told that there is a train from Buenos Aires to Santiago. I intend to take that train tomorrow," I said. "There is a problem, sir. You may try to stay here in Argentina." "Why would I? I have a visa to Chile, as you can see. My parents have been waiting for me for years." "Nice story, but is it true? Your passport will be requisitioned until your train ticket to Chile is booked. Meanwhile, you will stay on the ship."

The ship emptied completely. All the passengers disembarked with their suitcases and packages after a ruthless customs check. Many had brought products from Europe to sell in Argentina at a premium, to help finance their first months in the new country: a musical instrument, a power tool, a camera, or a typewriter. Once the ship emptied, crews of workers came up to disassemble the bunkbeds and prepare the ship for its return to Europe loaded with grains and meat. By evening, all had left. Only one guard remained, for the sole purpose of watching me.

I felt uneasy without my passport. Without a passport you are nobody; you don't have a name, you don't have a country, you do not exist. I did not know how long it would take the Argentinian officers to book my train ticket. I had no choice but to walk back and forth on the ship's deck and watch the hustle and bustle of the harbor from afar. I greeted the guard on the dock.

After six-thirty the guard became increasingly restless. He looked at his watch, walked to the end of the dock, and returned. "The night-shift guard has not arrived," he explained to me. At eight o'clock my guard left without his replacement having shown up. Based on my experience in Brazil, I decided to leave the ship to explore the great city of Buenos Aires. Nobody noticed as I left.

A friend had given me the address of his uncle, who owned a store in downtown Buenos Aires, so I decided to go there. I was mesmerized. I had never seen a city so illuminated and active in the late-night hours. Compared with war-ravaged European cities, this city was shining bright. The streets were packed with people, the retail stores and coffee houses were all open, and multitudes were flocking in and out of the many theaters lining the famous Florida street.

The uncle's store sold leather goods, wallets, purses, and belts. A chubby, bald man was attending to a client. I waited until he had completed the sale and then addressed him in Yiddish, telling him I brought greetings from his nephew. He looked at me surprised and suspicious. I explained who I was. The man came out from behind the counter to give me a hug, and then gave quick instructions to the store clerk and pushed me out to a café across the street. "Tell me, tell me everything," he begged. He had fled Germany to Argentina ten years earlier, while his sister fled to Palestine with her son, my friend. Letters had been their only contact, but now here I was, bringing direct regards from his family. Everything I told him seemed too little.

Shortly before midnight he crossed the street to close his store. "My wife has to meet you too. Come again tomorrow," he said. "If the guard is not at the dock, I will surely do so," I said, and left to immerse myself in the intense nightlife of this big city. At four in the morning, I returned to the ship. Nobody was on guard. The next morning, I waved to the day guard from the ship's deck; he was delighted to see me where I belonged. That night, his replacement failed to show up again, and I left to visit the city again.

On the third day the immigration police finally came to take me to the train station to continue my trip to Chile. "And my passport?" I asked. "We will return it to you at the border with Chile."

At the train station there was a crowd carrying garlands, flags, and banners with the phrase "Perón is with the Shirtless." They were celebrating the recent nationalization of the railways by Argentina's populist president Juan Perón. For over a century the railways had been owned by the British and the French, playing a crucial role in transforming Argentina into a prosperous producer and exporter to European markets. As ideologies of national self-determination expanded across the world, in Argentina the railways were a symbol of foreign control and became a target of Perón's government.

I was assigned to a train seat next to a man who did not speak during the whole trip. He may have been there just to ensure that I crossed to Chile. Once we arrived at the city of Mendoza, I changed to the Transandine Railway. This amazing railway followed an ancient, narrow 250-kilometer-long mule route across the majestic high Andean mountains, rising to 3,200 meters and passing through several long tunnels as it meandered along the mountain's edge to the town of Los Andes in Chile.

The train was packed full of people. It was the end of the summer holidays and vacationers were returning home. A group of five happy and boisterous young women invited me to sit with them. I did not understand a word of their Spanish, as they spoke very fast and with an accent that I was hearing for the first time. They soon taught two new terms: smuggling and customs. They were carrying tea which they wanted to sell later at a premium price to finance their vacation and asked me to carry some of their tea packs, as they knew the customs officials would be more lenient with a European. I also learned the lyrics of a trendy song the women sang over and over: *"La ultima noche que pase contigo"* [The last night I spent with you].

The customs official observed my tea packages; he then looked at the young women, suppressed a smile, and was satisfied. Not a hint of unnecessary inquisition. The Chilean police also gave me back my passport, saying: "Sir, welcome to Chile." I thought that this was a very nice beginning.

"This is this train's last station," the young women explained to me. "You now must switch to the north-south train to Santiago; we are switching too, so come with us." I dutifully followed them through the hustle and bustle and was soon seated on the new train waiting for departure.

I pondered. In a mere two hours I would meet my family. How would this reunion be, after ten years of separation? My parents would surely have aged visibly. My mother's health had deteriorated, and the challenges of immigration must have left deep traces in my father's face. And my sister, a 13-year-old girl when I left Germany, was now a woman. Would I even recognize her? And what about me? I was a schoolboy ten years ago, and now they would see a man hardened by life and war. What would this reunion be like?

Suddenly, I heard a faraway sound that shook me to my core: a familiar whistle from my childhood, the tune my father, my sister, and I whistled on our frequent treks in Germany. A sea of memories and emotions surged up. Who was whistling this familiar old melody in this unfamiliar train? The whistle came closer and closer. And there, walking along the train aisle, I saw an old man and a young woman whistling. My father? My sister?

"Vati!" I screamed, jumping out of my seat and running towards them. Oh God, what a moment that was! Hugs, kisses, tears, and wild emotions.

Unbeknownst to me, my parents and sister had decided to meet me in the town of Los Andes, rather than wait for hours in Santiago. They had searched for me on the station platform, in the customs room, in the officers' office, and everywhere, but could not find me. They thought I had failed to arrive; or maybe they could not recognize me at all, after so many years. They had only seen a few photographs of me in the last ten years. They really didn't know what I looked like... How would they find me? And then it occurred to them to call out to me with our old family whistling tune. What a joy, what a wealth of emotions!

My father and sister held me tightly, almost lifting me off the floor as they guided me to where Mutti was seated. More hugs, kisses, tears of emotion. The passengers participated in our joyful reunion as my mother cried and exclaimed in her broken Spanish: "My son, my son, ten years, ten years I have not seen my son!".

It was March 1, 1948. A decade-long life circle closed that day.

Onwards, onwards to a new life.

The Transandine Railway across the Andes mountains.

The murdered have no voice, the dead do not talk.
If we, the survivors, do not tell the story,
who will?

ACKNOWLEDGMENTS

I began writing my story in my seventies, initially, for my grandchildren. Throughout the years, many people helped transform it into this book. I never imagined that I would publish my war story to a world-wide audience in the year I turn 102 years old.

I thank all those who helped me in this process. It is impossible to name them all; to each of you who encouraged me, taught me, commented on my work, promoted my story, and invited me to speak, please receive my heartfelt thanks.

My writing mentor, the late author Carlos Cerda, guided me to improve my writing to create the story; my Literature Workshop companions helped with comments and friendship. Alberto Rojas, journalist, international analyst, and Director of the Observatorio de Asuntos Internacionales at Finis Terrae University, was key to push for the initial Spanish edition, which is the basis of this revised English edition. The Jewish community in Chile and friends have kept me active at this advanced age. Helen Fry, author, specialist in World War II British Intelligence, the Stiftung Exilmuseum Berlin, and the Stiftung Neue Synagoge Berlin, all interviewed me in 2022, which reaffirmed the interest in my story and encouraged my family to pursue the English edition.

My little family have been my strongest champions. My late wife Ati typed my initial handwritten manuscripts; my daughters Dalia and Liora have supported me, editing and translating the manuscript, organizing my speaking engagements, and running my social media. My grandchildren Tanya, Gadi, and Dan have been part of it all as well.

Lisa Malamud, Jonathan Newberg, Jim Beverley, and Tim Peck commented on the initial English draft. Luke Finley edited and cleaned up the final text. My special immense gratitude goes to Liesbeth Heenk of Amsterdam Publishers, for choosing to publish my story, and with it, provide a different perspective of Jewish history in World War II – that of a fighting Jew.

To all of you, thank you.

AMSTERDAM PUBLISHERS
HOLOCAUST LIBRARY

The series **Holocaust Survivor Memoirs World War II** consists of the following autobiographies of survivors:

Outcry. Holocaust Memoirs, by Manny Steinberg

Hank Brodt Holocaust Memoirs. A Candle and a Promise, by Deborah Donnelly

The Dead Years. Holocaust Memoirs, by Joseph Schupack

Rescued from the Ashes. The Diary of Leokadia Schmidt, Survivor of the Warsaw Ghetto, by Leokadia Schmidt

My Lvov. Holocaust Memoir of a twelve-year-old Girl, by Janina Hescheles

Remembering Ravensbrück. From Holocaust to Healing, by Natalie Hess

Wolf. A Story of Hate, by Zeev Scheinwald with Ella Scheinwald

Save my Children. An Astonishing Tale of Survival and its Unlikely Hero, by Leon Kleiner with Edwin Stepp

Holocaust Memoirs of a Bergen-Belsen Survivor & Classmate of Anne Frank, by Nanette Blitz Konig

Defiant German - Defiant Jew. A Holocaust Memoir from inside the Third Reich, by Walter Leopold with Les Leopold

In a Land of Forest and Darkness. The Holocaust Story of two Jewish Partisans, by Sara Lustigman Omelinski

Holocaust Memories. Annihilation and Survival in Slovakia, by Paul
Davidovits

From Auschwitz with Love. The Inspiring Memoir of Two Sisters'
Survival, Devotion and Triumph Told by Manci Grunberger Beran & Ruth
Grunberger Mermelstein, by Daniel Seymour

Remetz. Resistance Fighter and Survivor of the Warsaw Ghetto, by Jan
Yohay Remetz

My March Through Hell. A Young Girl's Terrifying Journey to Survival, by
Halina Kleiner with Edwin Stepp

Roman's Journey, by Roman Halter

Beyond Borders. Escaping the Holocaust and Fighting the Nazis. 1938 -
1948, by Rudi Haymann

The Engineers, by Henry Reiss

Memoirs by Elmar Rivosh, Sculptor (1906-1967). Riga Ghetto and Beyond,
by Elmar Rivosh

The series **Holocaust Survivor True Stories** consists of the following biographies:

Among the Reeds. The true story of how a family survived the Holocaust, by Tammy Bottner

A Holocaust Memoir of Love & Resilience. Mama's Survival from Lithuania to America, by Ettie Zilber

Living among the Dead. My Grandmother's Holocaust Survival Story of Love and Strength, by Adena Bernstein Astrowsky

Heart Songs. A Holocaust Memoir, by Barbara Gilford

Shoes of the Shoah. The Tomorrow of Yesterday, by Dorothy Pierce

Hidden in Berlin. A Holocaust Memoir, by Evelyn Joseph Grossman

Separated Together. The Incredible True WWII Story of Soulmates Stranded an Ocean Apart, by Kenneth P. Price, Ph.D.

The Man Across the River. The incredible story of one man's will to survive the Holocaust, by Zvi Wiesenfeld

If Anyone Calls, Tell Them I Died. A Memoir, by Emanuel (Manu) Rosen

The House on Thrömerstrasse. A Story of Rebirth and Renewal in the Wake of the Holocaust, by Ron Vincent

Dancing with my Father. His hidden past. Her quest for truth. How Nazi Vienna shaped a family's identity, by Jo Sorochinsky

The Story Keeper. Weaving the Threads of Time and Memory - A Memoir, by Fred Feldman

Krisia's Silence. The Girl who was not on Schindler's List, by Ronny Hein

Defying Death on the Danube. A Holocaust Survival Story, by Debbie J. Callahan with Henry Stern

A Doorway to Heroism. A decorated German-Jewish Soldier who became an American Hero, by Rabbi W. Jack Romberg

The Shoemaker's Son. The Life of a Holocaust Resister, by Laura Beth Bakst

The Redhead of Auschwitz. A True Story, by Nechama Birnbaum

Land of Many Bridges. My Father's Story, by Bela Ruth Samuel Tenenholtz

Creating Beauty from the Abyss. The Amazing Story of Sam Herciger, Auschwitz Survivor and Artist, by Lesley Ann Richardson

On Sunny Days We Sang. A Holocaust Story of Survival and Resilience, by Jeannette Grunhaus de Gelman

Painful Joy. A Holocaust Family Memoir, by Max J. Friedman

I Give You My Heart. A True Story of Courage and Survival, by Wendy Holden

In the Time of Madmen, by Mark A. Prelas

Monsters and Miracles. Horror, Heroes and the Holocaust, by Ira Wesley Kitmacher

Flower of Vlora. Growing up Jewish in Communist Albania, by Anna Kohen

Aftermath: Coming of Age on Three Continents. A Memoir, by Annette Libeskind Berkovits

Not a real Enemy. The True Story of a Hungarian Jewish Man's Fight for Freedom, by Robert Wolf

Zaidy's War. Four Armies, Three Continents, Two Brothers. One Man's Impossible Story of Endurance, by Martin Bodek

The Glassmaker's Son. Looking for the World my Father left behind in Nazi Germany, by Peter Kupfer

The Apprentice of Buchenwald. The True Story of the Teenage Boy Who Sabotaged Hitler's War Machine, by Oren Schneider

Good for a Single Journey, by Helen Joyce

Burying the Ghosts. She escaped Nazi Germany only to have her life torn apart by the woman she saved from the camps: her mother, by Sonia Case

American Wolf. From Nazi Refugee to American Spy. A True Story, by Audrey Birnbaum

Bipolar Refugee. A Saga of Survival and Resilience, by Peter Wiesner

Before the Beginning and After the End, by Hymie Anisman

The series **Jewish Children in the Holocaust** consists of the following autobiographies of Jewish children hidden during WWII in the Netherlands or Belgium:

Searching for Home. The Impact of WWII on a Hidden Child, by Joseph Gosler

See You Tonight and Promise to be a Good Boy! War memories, by Salo Muller

Sounds from Silence. Reflections of a Child Holocaust Survivor, Psychiatrist and Teacher, by Robert Krell

Sabine's Odyssey. A Hidden Child and her Dutch Rescuers, by Agnes Schipper

The Journey of a Hidden Child, by Harry Pila and Robin Black

The series **New Jewish Fiction** consists of the following novels, written by Jewish authors. All novels are set in the time during or after the Holocaust.

The Corset Maker. A Novel, by Annette Libeskind Berkovits

Escaping the Whale. The Holocaust is over. But is it ever over for the next generation? by Ruth Rotkowitz

When the Music Stopped. Willy Rosen's Holocaust, by Casey Hayes

Hands of Gold. One Man's Quest to Find the Silver Lining in Misfortune, by Roni Robbins

The Girl Who Counted Numbers. A Novel, by Roslyn Bernstein

There was a garden in Nuremberg. A Novel, by Navina Michal Clemerson

The Butterfly and the Axe, by Omer Bartov

To Live Another Day. A Novel, Elizabeth Rosenberg

A Worthy Life. Based on a True Story, by Dahlia Moore

The series **Holocaust Heritage** consists of the following memoirs by 2G:

The Cello Still Sings. A Generational Story of the Holocaust and of the
Transformative Power of Music, by Janet Horvath

The Fire and the Bonfire. A Journey into Memory, by Ardyn Halter

The Silk Factory: Finding Threads of My Family's True Holocaust Story,
by Michael Hickins

The series **Holocaust Books for Young Adults** consists of the following
novels, based on true stories:

The Boy behind the Door. How Salomon Kool Escaped the Nazis.
Inspired by a True Story, by David Tabatsky

Running for Shelter. A True Story, by Suzette Sheft

The Precious Few. An Inspirational Saga of Courage based on True
Stories, by David Twain with Art Twain

The series **WWII Historical Fiction** consists of the following novels, some of which are based on true stories:

Mendelevski's Box. A Heartwarming and Heartbreaking Jewish Survivor's Story, by Roger Swindells

A Quiet Genocide. The Untold Holocaust of Disabled Children in WWII Germany, by Glenn Bryant

The Knife-Edge Path, by Patrick T. Leahy

Brave Face. The Inspiring WWII Memoir of a Dutch/German Child, by I. Caroline Crocker and Meta A. Evenbly

When We Had Wings. The Gripping Story of an Orphan in Janusz Korczak's Orphanage. A Historical Novel, by Tami Shem-Tov

Jacob's Courage. Romance and Survival amidst the Horrors of War, by Charles S. Weinblatt

Want to be an AP book reviewer?

Reviews are very important in a world dominated by the social media and social proof.

Please drop us a line if you want to join the *AP review team* and show us at least one review already posted on Amazon for one of our books.

info@amsterdampublishers.com